Some Delights of the Hudson Valley

For Dirk

REJECTED COVER

A Man Walks Into A River...

Dear Danny —
Sorry, have to reject this — not quite funny enough.
Best of Luck,
Danny

An Anthology of Hudson Valley Humor

Compiled & Edited by Danny Shanahan

Shanahan

Epigraph
Rhinebeck · New York

Peter McCarty

Table Of Contents

Joy Taylor

From the Editor

WHEN I WAS TWO YEARS OLD, my family and I lived in a fourth floor walk-up in Brooklyn. It was located in one of the Heights, Prospect I think, or possibly Wuthering. One lazy Saturday afternoon, lulled by the heat and humidity, the hypnotic motion of my mother ironing a full laundry basket of dad's cravats caused me to swoon. I fell backwards, taking a tumble out of an open window. My mom's panicked screams rocked the neighborhood. Madame Novatna, the fortuneteller on the first floor, immediately dialed 911, although this service wouldn't be invented for another thirty years (she was that good). Fortunately, I was unhurt, having landed on an elderly woman walking a jaguar cub. This was a defining moment in my life. Although my mother was in hysterics, I was laughing hysterically. The gathering crowd, realizing I had emerged unscathed, laughed too. A bit nervously, perhaps, because it seemed like the old woman and the big cat might be down for the count. To me, it couldn't have been funnier, not even if I had landed on a capybara, the largest rodent in the world, and the sworn mortal enemy of the jaguar. But hey, a capybara? It's not like we lived in Manhattan!

Since that fateful day I've treasured humor above all things. A sense of humor is what sets us apart from the lesser beasts, the birds of the field, the avenging angels, the boy wizards. A sense of humor is what lead me to my eventual career choice, funny bartender, and then, finally, *New Yorker* cartoonist. And a sense of humor is why, having edited 400* books of my own cartoons, I was asked to pull together the collection you now hold in your hands. My assignment? Contact varied and interesting contributors living or working in this area we love, the Hudson Valley, then beg them to come up with funny material. The response was truly astounding, even to a jaded jaguar man like myself.

---

* Actually four, but 400 is a nicer number. And who reads footnotes, anyway?

The brilliant conductor/writer/college president Leon Botstein is here, along with the legendary singer/songwriter/rocker Graham Parker. Writer/poet/ professor Robert Kelly shares a laugh, as does (out of slashes—must use alliteration) local literary luminary Mary Gaitskill, chiming in with a truly hilarious cartoon (who knew?). We have stars of stage and screen: Denny Dillon, Mary Louise Wilson, and Lou Trapani, to name a few. Rounding things out is a bevy of cartoonists and writers, artists, and poets, and whether you prefer a sly, knowing grin, a satisfied chuckle, or a full-out braying guffaw, all will make you laugh.

So enjoy already. And don't forget to tip your bartender.

Danny Shanahan

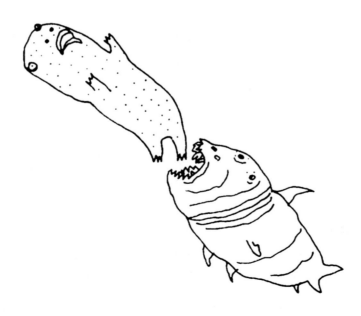

Untitled

Leon Botstein

THE HUDSON VALLEY HAS THE PECULIAR VIRTUE of making its inhabitants forget that they are not living in a city. Those of us who grew up in New York City and continued our education in Chicago and Boston, and therefore never tasted rural life until adulthood, made the decision to live outside a city with considerable trepidation. At some time in our education we'd absorbed the vulgar Marxist idea that there's something idiotic about rural life, something vaguely primitive and antimodern. Some individuals flee the cities because they are impersonal, difficult to manage, ugly, and polluted. But there are those of us who love the smell of the street and don't mind the smog and the noise, and are frightened more by birds and the wind than by garbage trucks, ambulance sirens, honking horns, and imposing skyscrapers. For those of us who had contemporaries who pioneered a back-to-the-land movement and embraced wood-burning stoves and a premodern lifestyle, there was an inner resistance to joining that all-too-romantic and sentimental movement.

But the Hudson Valley is the ideal illusionistic compromise. One can live an entirely civilized life and never step on anything but concrete and asphalt. There is a great college and a fine library here at Bard and all the riches of culture that we associate with a city. Our neighbors include artists, writers, scholars, musicians, and people in government and public service with high ambition and the capacity for fine and original conversation. One can feel at home without hiking, kayaking, running, walking, or bird watching, much less farming or gardening. By ignoring all the evident rural aspects of the Hudson Valley, I've come to appreciate their beauties at a safe distance. One gets used to the clean air, the trees, the magnificent river, and the aging mountains once inhabited by borscht belt comedians as well as old WASP families ensconced in storybook-like camps that reveal the snobbery of faded elegance.

But the three most remarkable things about the Hudson Valley are the balance it strikes between past and present, the ease and civility it offers in the conduct of daily life, and most importantly, the sense of commonality it fosters among its inhabitants. There are buildings by A. J. Davis, outsized and often-rundown mansions on the river, and the homes of Eleanor and Franklin Roosevelt. One can catch glimpses of a Dutch and English colonial past, and the patterns of tourism of the early twentieth century. There even are nostalgic reminders of the 1950s, particularly the A. L. Stickles department store in Rhinebeck. These layers of the past stand seamlessly alongside the trailer parks, malls, charming but unplanned buildings, housing garages, movie houses, and restaurants that have sprung up during the past forty years. There are thankfully also towering glimpses of the contemporary, including the magnificent Frank Gehry–designed Fisher Center for the Performing Arts and Rafael Vinoly's new science center on the Bard campus as well as a few hyper-modern homes tucked away in the woods. Normally that balance can be found only in a city, but it thrives in the Hudson Valley.

After living for decades in the Hudson Valley, I've come to realize that cities eat up your time. Not only is it painfully difficult to do the basic shopping and dry cleaning, but it is impossible to get a washing machine fixed or a watch repaired within a reasonable time period. In the Hudson Valley every convenience one would want is easily accessible, and the people who provide the services are polite and personal in their interactions. Standing in line at Holy Cow, home of the best soft ice cream in the world, one almost feels as if one is somewhere in Garrison Keillor's backyard in the neighborliness and kindnesses that inform the everyday. If one is a musician or a scholar, or an artist or a writer, you'll get ten times as much work done living here. In most of our cities we're overwhelmed by the temptation to consume rather than to produce work, and by unspoken pretensions about what one has seen or not seen, which restaurant one has frequented, and whom one knows. There is no reigning society here, no arrogant plutocracy, no captains of industry.

And this brings us to the final virtue of the Hudson Valley: its people. If America has redeeming virtues, they rest in the belief in a gracious egalitarianism. We feel few distinctions living here based on wealth and privilege. We break bread and argue with individuals with radically different political beliefs—in my case, hardheaded Republicans—without too much acrimony and mistrust. The students at Bard, who come from all over the world and from all over the nation, readily feel at home and welcome. It is a joy to see the Red Hook High School band and chorus perform on the stage of one of the most beautiful and acoustically perfect concert halls in the world and to see how well they acquit themselves. Surprisingly enough, there's nothing too Peyton Place about the region, just enough to permit the desirable level of gossip (an essential human experience), as one walks into a restaurant and sees people one knows, chats with the owners of Northern Dutchess Pharmacy, and stops to talk with acquaintances on the street or at the IGA. The Hudson Valley is spread out enough, and there is enough separation between the small communities that make up the Hudson Valley. We experience the requisite dosage of anonymity and intimacy in a manner that makes a sense of claustrophobia or loneliness more rare than it otherwise might be. It's a great place where one can make one's mark in full confidence that one has no regrets about living in this day and age as opposed to some glorious moment in the past. The Hudson Valley is tailor-made for optimism about one's work, oneself, and one's family.

Michael Crawford

RHINEBECK RECORD
ESCAPES
EDDIE POUGHKEEP, 78, FLA. NATIVE, NEVER REALLY LIVED HERE
MURIEL CITRUS, 99, LONG CLAIMED 'NOT LONG FOR THIS WORLD', PROVEN WRONG
SHIRLEY LOX, 87, KNEW 'OF' FDR, NEVER FOUND THE PERFECT BAGEL
STAN PINK, 86, TIRELESS, HELIUM-VOICED VOICE OF REASON ON COUNCIL
BYRON ALIAS, 91, ODD FAMILY NAME MEANT MEATCUTTER FREQUENTLY HAD SOME EXPLAINING TO DO...
'ACE' AND FAY FINK, BOTH 88, SUCCUMB SIMULTANEOUSLY WHILE CELEBRATING GOLDEN ANNIVERSARY AT COSIMO'S ON RTE. 9
—MORE' ESCAPES IN SPORTS—

Up Among the Stars

Mary Louise Wilson

I WAS IN ECONOMY, in the aisle seat. Usually when I fly it's for a film job in which case I'm flown first class. This time, however, I was flying myself to the Virgin Islands.

The drinks cart slammed against me, causing me to drop my magazine and that's when I noticed this head of longish, wavy white hair sitting in first class. It looked so familiar. Suddenly I thought: that's the head of Donald Sutherland! I had worked with Donald Sutherland. In *Klute*. Well I didn't actually meet him because he wasn't in my scene. I was the lady in the store; my line was, "Hey, what happened?" Anyway, I fixated on that head for a long while, hoping it would turn so I could make a positive ID. But after a while I thought, so what if it is Donald Sutherland, big deal, he's just a passenger trying to enjoy his trip, like the rest of us. I went back to my magazine and this fascinating article about disappearing ice caps.

When the seat belt sign finally went off, I needed a restroom. Food carts were blocking the aisle toward the back, so I was forced to walk forward, to the restroom in first class. Of course, once up there I couldn't very well avoid glancing over at the white head. I only needed to see a big ear, a steely blue eye and half a carved upper lip, and I said to myself, that is Donald Sutherland sitting there. I used the restroom and returned to my seat.

The stewardesses were taking lunch orders. I ended up with "strip steak," a grey slab with a side order of four uncooked green beans and a yellow ball of something that tasted like ammonia. We had barely finished eating when the loudspeaker told us to sit back and enjoy the movie. The tray tables were slammed shut, window shades yanked down and the curtain between economy and first class closed.

The movie was *Titanic*. I intended to watch but kept dozing off. Every now and then screams woke me and I glimpsed Kate Winslet floating around her stateroom or Leonardo DiCaprio stuffing his jacket in a porthole, or side-stroking through the dining saloon. I wondered what Donald was watching. Did they get a different movie, a first release, perhaps?

By the way, besides *Klute*, I played the secretary in the limo in *Everybody Wins*, the lady at the party who took her bra off in *Mr. Wonderful*, and the nosy neighbor in a scene with Burt Reynolds in *Best Little Whorehouse*.

When the movie ended there was a mass exodus into the aisles and lines formed for restrooms fore and aft. A man in an undershirt and cutoffs barged into first class and leaned on the back of Donald's seat! I loathe people like that. I would never do that, even though Donald and I are in the same business. Donald was the complete gentleman, smiling and nodding as if he couldn't think of anything he'd rather do than chat it up with this balding clown in cutoffs.

The plane finally landed. I was nervous about making my connecting flight, but I got there in plenty of time. The boarding area was deserted. I looked around and there, in the middle of a sea of empty seats, was Donald and his travel companion, Mrs. Sutherland, I suppose. He was sitting there surrounded by various carryons, reading a book. I couldn't believe he was just sitting there like that, completely exposed to any passing bozo. I deliberately chose a seat a few rows away. I behaved perfectly normally, arranged my coat on the chair, inspected my shoes and only occasionally glanced in their general direction, looking for a clock or something. I felt that by sitting more or less in their vicinity I could somehow protect them from wandering autograph nuts. But sure enough, before very long this man comes up to Donald and I'm thinking, for God's sake leave the poor guy alone, when Donald and Mrs. Sutherland gathered up all their things and followed the man down the corridor. He was obviously some sort of airport official and of course he was escorting them to some sort of VIP lounge to wait for their flight. That made sense.

I thought, well that's that, but an hour later as I was walking out onto the tarmac toward the small plane bound for St. John's I spotted Donald and his wife walking ahead of me. I hoped he didn't think I was following them! I kept my eyes averted; I studied my ticket, the bleached landscape, the stewardess, as we climbed the metal stairs and entered the small cabin. Donald was sitting three seats ahead of me. I could have reached out and patted his head.

And then, almost as soon as we were in the air, the ride got rough. The plane was bouncing around, drinks were spilling and the stewardess was staggering and falling onto the passengers. We weren't going to make it; people starting moaning and then the pilots voice informed us that he was going to make a forced landing. We jounced and lurched and dropped and dropped, and then the plane touched down and bounced once, twice, and then skidded at top speed along the ground, the wind screeching, passengers screaming, headed straight for a grove of trees, and then, blackout. We crashed, they started pulling those that were hurt out of the cabin. I was one of those; I was carried half conscious and laid out on the ground. People bent over me; I was trying to say something. He couldn't hear me. A man put his ear to my lips; "What is it? What are you trying to say?" And with the last breath in my body, I gasped, "Tell Donald Sutherland I was in *Klute* too!"

This Kid of Mine

Mark Burns

HE IS REALLY SOMETHING, this kid of mine. So the fifth graders were supposed to complete some kind of science project and he was wondering what to do. Avoiding it really, like kids do, but not just because he's bored of the same old crap. Frankly, at eleven, he's old for his age, ahead of the curve in the learning department, if you know what I mean. Doesn't test well, but a ton of smarts.

"Why not do your project about how electricity works or something?" I make the mistake of asking him.

"Why don't you go sit on it and rotate?" he says, stubbing out his cigarette on the arm of the sofa. Which is really okay because it's old anyway and I should have gotten a new one a long time ago. Still, I was about to say something about his attitude, but he got a phone call from his girlfriend, Louisa. She may be eight years older than him, but she doesn't act like it. Talk about immature!

Long story short, next day I had this recurring sharp pain in my side, so I go to the doctor who tells me it's my gall bladder. I don't even know where the hell it is or what it does, but according to him it's got to come out. "Not a difficult operation, any surgeon could do it with his eyes closed," he says. Before I can even think of any questions to ask, he's on his way to some pharmaceutical convention in Tonga.

Back home I'm doubled over in pain when my sister calls and I have to hear about what a brain my nephew is. How he's number one in his class, president of the eighth grade, speaks Farsi, or some weird tongue, and plays an instrument called a "clavier." He also got admitted to a Yale summer program for gifted pre-engineering students and he's getting a free ride at one of those exclusive New England boarding schools next year. I think in his spare time he even found a cure for shingles.

While she yaps on and on, I'm getting ticked off and competitive. I start thinking about that science project. And that's when it hits me that my kid should take my gall bladder out.

Once he realized I wasn't kidding, he jumped at the idea. He's no slouch, this kid of mine, which is hard to explain to his teachers when they ask why he cuts school so much, never does his homework, and fails most of his tests. How about you give him something challenging to do for once!

It amazes me, the things kids can get off the Internet. He finds a website that not only shows you step-by-step how to take out a gall bladder, but they even sell you the tools to do it. Sure, it was from overseas, written in Chinese, but it didn't matter because all he had to do was use one of those on-line translators (which makes you wonder why we need all these overpaid foreign-language teachers in our schools!). "Gall bladder take-out easy as dumplings."

He certainly did his homework (ironically!) before the operation. As he explained it to me, the gall bladder is basically this Tianjin Province–shaped organ (like a pear) near the liver. It collects and stores bile—green stuff that helps you digest food. I had gallstones. I don't know how the hell I caught them, but they blocked my bile and that's not a good thing, so the bladder had to go. What kills me is that you don't even really need this organ. My kid said it's as if one of those useless cable channels in the one-hundreds that you never asked for and never watch is suddenly responsible for screwing up all your TV reception.

He found the anesthesiologist on Craigslist: Doctor "Deep Rem." (At first I thought he was from India.) Technically speaking, he's a former anesthesiologist. Sure, he'd lost his medical license in Florida, which is really difficult to do, but he quoted us a good price, and a phone call to his parole officer verified that he had indeed completed a substance-abuse recovery program and 1,000 hours of community service in Sarasota. You have to admire a guy for that.

The kid "scored" the various medicinal necessities off a Canadian website. He asked Louisa to assist him during the operation because she has "good hands and a strong stomach" (he met her when she was working at a tattoo parlor). She was also able to squeeze into a cute nurse's outfit she had left over from last Halloween. I tell you, she looked about five inches taller in those white platforms.

Things went fairly well, though I guess at the critical moment when he was about to cut the "cystic artery" he looks up and sees Louisa face-flirting with Dr. Rem. He told me he thought about stabbing the "Doc" with a scalpel, but he stayed cool because he wasn't sure he'd be able to get me out of the anesthesia by himself. Louisa sewed me up after and did a great job. She said it was nothing compared to the time she had to ink a peacock on the bald head of her Special Forces ex-boyfriend the night before he went off to Afghanistan.

The only thing my kid didn't do was sterilize the instruments, which I had reminded him about probably fifty times before the surgery. If you've ever tried to get your kid to do the dishes, you know how that goes! Come to think of it, I'll bet he didn't even wash his hands. Sometimes you just want to strangle them, right?

I'm sure that's why, beyond the usual postsurgery pain from trauma and tugging of stitches when I so much as coughed, suddenly I was spiking a fever of 105 degrees. He's got good instincts, guesses infection and pumps me full of what he thought was antibiotics. Only turns out it's cut-rate Viagra, due to some mix-up with the Canadian supplier. He figured it out when he realized I was "tent-poling" my blanket for more than six hours while I was lying on my back shivering like an overloaded washing machine. (It was pretty embarrassing to see myself like that on YouTube!) Once he got the real stuff into me I was fine after a few weeks.

Good news is he got an "A" on his science project, though his teacher didn't believe him until he showed her the video and a jar with my bladder floating in it. (We should have kept it in the refrigerator—what a stink!)

Sad news is Louisa left my boy for Dr. Deep Rem. I told him she wasn't good enough for him, but I know it still hurt. He'll bounce back. He's resilient, not to mention self-motivated. Our neighbor, a woman who works at the convenience store, doesn't have health insurance and she needs a hip replacement. Piece of cake for this kid of mine.

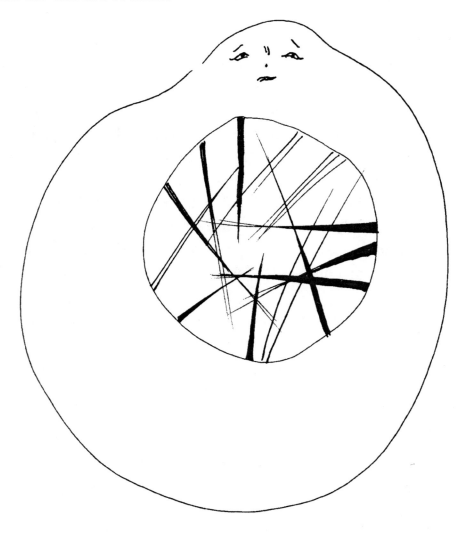

I've had better days.

Jillen Lowe

A Tale of Two Pickelhaubes

Wade Rubenstein

W E TOOK A BOOTH IN BLONDE PETER'S, an old diner on Main in Kaiser's Ravine. To outsiders, we looked like a pair of locals, dressed as we were in our spiffy Pickelhaubes—the Prussian-blue hats with metal spikes favored by our Hudson Valley burg. But to those born and raised here and descended from pioneering Palatine settlers—volk whose Pickelhaubes bore the scuffs of centuries—we were nothing but wanabees, no better than the tourists.

Yes, we pseudo-locals would be served at Blonde Peters, as Kaiser's Ravine was renowned for its hospitality (not to mention its gold-lettered shops with their love of Visa-Gold), but service wasn't to be confused with acceptance. In fact, as our waitress, Kaiser Wilhelm VIII, or "Kaisie," for short, and she was (but plucky!), came to take our order, Blonde Peter himself spied us from the counter, where he coolly rubbed salve into a dueling scar. The scar was said to be a souvenir from a tourist whose scrambled eggs arrived runny—an intolerable insult to men from northern New Jersey.

"Brunch, gentlemen?" Kaisie asked us, pen ready, a smirk affixed to her full lips.

I glanced across the table at my well-tanned companion, Manny Hamasham (Man-Ham to friends and family), to see if he was any closer to making a selection than me. He pushed back the visor of his Pickelhaube and patted his belly before ordering the Schnitzelgruben Deluxe (good value—it comes with a side of knockwurst) and a peppermint schnapps on the rocks; an odd breakfast to the uninitiated, perhaps, but I've heard of odder, and besides, when in Kaiser's Ravine, I guess....

"Your wife told me you're supposed to lay off the knockwurst," I said, affecting a semi-solemn look.

"Not at all. I ordered it for you."

"Thanks."

"Besides, what's a couple of knockwursts among friends?"

"Okay," I told him, "just promise me no more knock-knock swordfights. It's been done."

"Don't remind me," said Man-Ham, who raised three fingers. "Scout's honor," he said.

"Hey, there's an oath that lends confidence," said I.

"And for you?" Kaisie asked me, her smirk falling open, the back of her pen pressed against her bottom lip.

"Ever tried Blonde Peter's gas-oven potatoes?" Man-Ham asked me, a single bushy eyebrow rising.

"No, I'm afraid I wouldn't like them."

"Maybe not," Man-Ham said, shrugging.

"Are we getting close?" said Kaisie, scanning her other customers before gazing back at me.

"Sorry. Let's see—I'll have the Bavarian Waffle Brunch, with gooseberries, please. That that comes with und stein of Budveiser, ya?"

"Ah, Budveiser—das Fuehrer of Beers," said Man-Ham, nodding approval as we handed our menus back to Kaisie, both of us smiling at her in a pathetic attempt at ingratiation.

"Thank you gentlemen," said Kaisie, and she marched back to the kitchen.

From his lap, Man-Ham pulled out a sketchbook and pen and laid them on his Rhineland! placemat. He looked at me, blue eyes glinting with mischief, when bells jingled and the Mayor swaggered in (if the profoundly bow-legged can be said to swagger). At the sight of us plotting over Man-Ham's sketchbook, the Mayor rattled his saber, twitching it in that inimical way of men born with insufficient penis. Blonde Peter left his stool for the Mayor, hand extended. "Herr Bürgermeister, always an honor to see you."

The Mayor pulled Blonde Peter aside for a word. Each raised a furtive monocle in our direction.

Watching them, Man-Ham laughed a bit uncomfortably. In a low voice, he said, "I hope they don't ficken my schnitzelgruben."

"Do you think they would?"

"How would I know if they did?"

"Good point. So, you said you had an idea for a screenplay?" I asked, hoping to launch the project Man-Ham proposed on the phone.

Man-Ham grinned, drawing pictures to outline an island, a bonfire, a portly accountant roasting on a spit. Pointing at his drawings like an admiral, he said, "When I was in Martha's Vineyard I imagined an island in the Atlantic near... HERE." He rapped the map he'd drawn with his spoon, drawing looks from around the diner. "And let's say that the Palatines settled that island centuries ago, just like they did in Kaiser's Ravine. Today, this island seems as peaceful as Vineyard Haven. But originally, those settlers struggled to the point where they cannibalized each other—the sick, the weak, the well-marbled went first. And because the struggles lasted for generations, their descendants acquired a taste for human flesh. To this day, dozens of tourists disappear each year, leaving nothing behind but a whiff of barbecue sauce. I'm thinking we'd call the island, the screenplay, Cannibal Run. What do you think?"

Not hearing any footsteps, but something almost like a stillborn scream, I looked up to find Kaisie standing an awkward distance from our table.

"Your drinks, gentlemen," she said, lunging forward, rapping the schnapps and beer on the table, spilling both, before serving our food. She seemed to squelch another yelp as she set it down.

"Careful, boys," she told us. "Hot plates."

"Um, thanks," said Man-Ham, giving me the "what's-wrong-with-her look," which I returned in kind, watching Kaisie dash over to Blonde Peter and the Mayor.

Frowning, I looked back at Man-Ham. "Cannibals? Too highbrow for me. What about an island called Martha Stewart's Haven? A prison island where convicts are forced to survive without sunscreen?"

"Sigh," said Man-Ham, before chewing a forkful of schnitzelgruben.

"How is it?" I asked, spearing a knockwurst, myself.

"A little gamey, today."

"That's strange, so's this," I said, looking up as Kaisie interrupted her boss's conversation. Nodding toward us, her mouth formed two distinct words, "They know." Both men then turned and glared. The Bürgermeister worked at his saber.

"For God's sake, hold onto your Pickelhaube and run," said Man-Ham, gripping his helmet.

"You think? Everybody knows the Bürgermeister's got no blade."

"Just kidding. Let's order dessert," said Man-Ham. "Where's Kaisie? I could use another schnapps."

Marmota Monax
Sampling J. Burroughs

Jane Heidgerd

WHISTLE-PIG OR GROUNDHOG, the woodchuck
is a rodent, related to the squirrel and rat
more of the field than the woods
a ravenous eater of grass, garden morsels, anything good
still, they avoid us with every step, and for all their exercise
you never see one fit and trim
just how does the female choose him?
A bag of bowels encased in fur, he spends
half the year sleeping, and the other gorging
vegetarian, and yet his meat is the smelliest
that only the starving would eat, and many predators decline
in favor of raw root.

What then, does the common woodchuck do
to deserve such groundedness?
Bask in the sun.
Double their weight and run, waddling.

Look, there goes another one from my neighbor's yard
in the pest-controller's cage.

A pest is a pest, but who's best
that groundhog or the skunk who's moving in?

Liza Donnelly

"BUT DAD, YOU SAID WHEN THE TREE HOUSE WAS FINISHED, WE COULD HAVE IT."

Drawing Advice 101

Render Stetson-Shanahan

THE SCRATCHING OF GRAPHITE ON PAPER suddenly slows, then stops completely, and the table shifts a little when he leans over and says, "How am I supposed to draw the nose when it's pointed right at me? How do you deal with the nostrils?" It's a hard angle, I tell him, leaning the other way to get a better look at the glossy image he's transcribing. The paper slides to me and I make a few quick light marks above the philtrum. That's one way to do it. In a moment the dashes get traced darkly as if they are being cemented in perfection, yet they were really just meant as minor suggestions. One more five-minute silence is followed by another how do I do that? And the paper slides over again. It's not that I don't like to give tips, but every so often someone will continue asking for the best technique without even realizing it, and at some point, I'd rather just sketch the face and leave out the easy parts, if the final product is so much more interesting than the process. Whoa, you did that really quickly. Are you even trying? Do you practice much? Are you better than your dad? These are some favorite follow-ups.

I never answer them very well, probably because none of them are really great questions. Speed doesn't matter. Gaudi started the Sagrada Familia in 1882: He's dead, and it won't be done until 2026, at least. But it looks sweet. Am I trying? It would be odd to look down from time to time to find that I've painted something intricate on a table, or my arm, or my dog's forehead. It doesn't happen, so yes, I have to try a little. Practice?

Every time I draw, I'm practicing. How often? Look at the backsides of the all the papers in my calculus binder. Every time I get the dad question, I want to look at the person intensely and whisper, Yeah, we have matches after dinner on the weekend. Last Friday, he won all three rounds, but this week we're doing North American birds of prey, so I feel like I have a pretty good chance. If you really want decent drawing advice, make the question more open ended, less specific. Instead of, How do I approach this body part, ask, What is it that I'm not doing in the first place? Teach a man how to fish, show a man how to fish, and all that. If I got a question that broad, I might actually have to think about it for a minute. Have more confidence with line; try not to erase so much. Make a grounding outline, and stick to it. Spend more time on details. Develop your own approach, a unique style. Stop using a sharpie. These are all better answers than, "Here, let me do it."

I haven't heard an inquiry in awhile, so I flick my eyeballs at his paper. Strokes tumble out of an indecisive pencil. Smudged, streaked, carved, retraced. Little shreds of eraser encircle the perimeter like miniature pink pedestrians watching a street brawl that has broken out between the pencil tip and the paper, recording it on their cell phones. All at once he throws down the pencil and slides the paper at me. Just, just, just, could you just draw this one part? I feel like I should deal out some lasting advise, but instead I just retrace the jaw line. He doesn't even watch. I send it back down the line. He snatches it, folds it, and tosses it into the trash. "Screw this, I'm bored. Can I flip through your calc binder?"

Random Tales of Times Gone By

Only the names are changed to protect the guilty!

Jay Dorin

SOMETIMES I THINK THE FUNNIEST TIMES of my life took place during the years of high school. There was something happening that cracked you up every single day. It was the days of fall down, lose control laughing. I wish I could remember everything that happened, but at this time of life I'm glad I remember anything.

We fade to a quiet Monday in September when Ray Carluccio, the very person who introduced me to the intrusive art of crank calling, said in a rather concerned voice, "You wouldn't believe what happened in my house yesterday afternoon!"

And thus was born...........

The Saga of Mr. Carluccio's Cat

It was an extremely warm fall day and in 1958 most of us poor New Yorkers could never afford the luxury of air conditioning. Ray's dad was a rather large man tipping the scales at close to 300 pounds. He decided that Sunday afternoon that it was a bit too hot to do anything else but just remove his clothes, get off his feet, lay on the couch, watch a little baseball, and indulge in a fine fifty-cent cigar.

The ball game was boring, the couch comfortable, and the warm room provided the perfect environment for Mr. Carluccio to nod off. As he did, he felt the lit cigar roll from his finger tips under the marble table. "Ah shit," he mumbled. Moving from the couch to the other side of the marble table, Mr. Carluccio began crawling under the table so as to retrieve the lit cigar. Ray's cat Frisky was also sitting by the marble table. She was carefully watching as Mr. Carluccio maneuvered his rather large frame under the soon-to-be famous table. It was actually Mr. Carluccio's well-exposed balls that reminded her of her favorite fuzzy toy and piqued Frisky's feline curiosity. Within a split second she took a grand swipe at his rather large "boys" and landed a direct and savage hit with all claws. A great scream welled from the depths of Mr. Carluccio while four thin lines of blood appeared where none had ever appeared before. Mr. Carluccio bolted upward, smashing his head on the underside of the table and knocking himself unconscious. Within seconds the living room was full of family members. Mr. Carluccio's now-stilled body lay quietly under the marble table, a thin trickle of blood coming from his slightly injured balls as well as his slightly injured head. Ray's mother was screaming for Ralph to call an ambulance while Frisky, the beloved family cat, just sat and watched, curious about all the commotion.

The ambulance attendants arrived promptly and with the help of all concerned lifted the large and semiconscious Mr. Carluccio up on the stretcher. Carefully and with the deftness of piano movers he was placed safely in the ambulance. Mr. Carluccio was transported to Coney Island Hospital where his wounds both top and bottom were cleaned and swabbed and checked for damage. Later that evening he returned home slightly bandaged, slightly embarrassed, and slightly dressed. Ray had now become one story richer and generously shared the wealth with all who were around to listen.

Frisky? Well what about Frisky? She was never heard from again. Nah, I'm just kidding.

Carluccio's best friend was Peter Buffalato. And thus begins the true tale of:

Buffalato's Amazing Machine

Nobody was having any real sex in high school in the '50s. Some guys said they were and maybe they were, but not anybody that I really knew, except my friend Kenny.

The closest thing to getting laid was masturbating and guys talked about that like they had the hottest girlfriend. Therefore, when Peter Buffalato proudly announced his invention of a jerk-off machine, it immediately commanded everyone's rapt attention. This was certainly an amazing thing, tantamount to inventing the wheel. Buffalato was all aglow with his new invention and immediately took the honor of local hero. We boys were excited beyond belief. There was no time to delay. Peter thusly informed us that Tuesday night was a good night to try out his machine.

When Wednesday arrived, Buffalato was notably absent. Thursday came and still no Buffalato. When Friday came and Peter B still was not in, we began to feel some concern. The weekend passed slowly and when Buffalato showed up Monday morning he appeared to be moving painfully slow. He courageously informed us he had been in the hospital due to an injury suffered at the hands of his amazing machine.

What he told us was this: His original brainstorm had occurred when down in his father's shop he was fixated on a machine that had three protruding metal rods that ran eccentrically rather than simply spinning. That is, when you turn the machine on the three rods, in the shape of a triangle-moved closer to each other and then apart. "Hmmmmm," thought the always deep-thinking Buffalato. "I know I have something here, but what?" The light went on. "If I put a roll of toilet paper on each rod they would squeeze together and then apart and just continue doing that. Kind of like sex." The concept was perfect. "I only have to wait for the right time," he thought.

Tuesday night rolled around and things were quiet upstairs. Peter stealthily advanced to the closet where the toilet paper was kept and quietly withdrew three rolls. Quietly he moved down the basement stairs, closing the door, advancing towards his machine.

The moment had arrived. He carefully placed a fresh roll on each of the protruding rods. He then grabbed a little stool to reach the correct height. Peter readied himself by staring at the centerfold of *Playboy*. He then placed his now excited organ in between the three newly papered rods and turned his mechanical lover's switch to the on position. That was his last conscious memory.

Peter, a true engineer, realized later that further preliminary tests would have been prudent. Everything in theory was excellent. However, when his amazing machine was turned on the rolls of toilet paper came together with such a tremendous crushing force that Peter was, so to speak, instantaneously extruded. Like every real man, the lower brain often rules. A pressure check would have certainly been a good idea.

Peter's parents found him lying on the floor, the stool overturned, his pants around his ankles, and the machine just humming along joyously, toilet paper intact around each rod, while Peter was quietly mumbling.

He awoke in a daze, in the emergency room of that same Coney Island Hospital, to the murmur of three doctors talking about how much "it" resembled a knitting needle.

Is there a moral to this story? Surely there is. But I haven't figured it out.

The Pearl

When we were kids, about the age of fourteen, James Munsey stuck a pearl up his nose. It was so far up that his mother had to take him to the emergency room at Medical Center on 168th Street to have it removed. The doctor very carefully extracted the pearl from James's nose and proudly returned it to him in a small container as a souvenir. While James and his mother were cabbing it back home to 156th Street, James removed the pearl from the vial and started rolling it around in between his fingers. One can only guess why, but if you knew James it was no surprise that he, quietly, during a meditative moment, stuck the pearl deep in his ear; so far in that neither he nor his mother could reach it and get it out. The cab made a quick U-turn and within minutes James was in the same emergency room seeing the same doctor who was fascinated with James's lack of clear thinking. This time the pearl was kept by the doctor, who felt he could not extract any more pearls from any other of James's orifices.

I also heard that James ran right through a wall in his house. He had a failure to turn in time.

The stories keep coming. Raymond Sysnofsky and the *Dog Shit Firecracker*, Raphael and Jorge Velez whose grandfather's ghostly presence used their bathroom the day after he passed away, Buffalo, crazy Vernon, Sonny Sanford, Joey Vega lighting his hair on fire at the disco.... And life on the block continues.

Graham Parker: The Lost Interview
By Jay Weinerbaum for Camper's Monthly

Graham Parker

I N THE FALL OF 1992, I caught up with veteran pub-rocker Graham Parker backstage at The Chance in Poughkeepsie to do an interview for *Camper's Monthly.*

Due to some new breakthroughs in guy rope technology, the editor had to shelve the piece, but now, some sixteen years later, thanks to the folks at my new place of employment, Roots Rocking Online, the interview is finally seeing the light of day!

Parker had recently moved to the Hudson Valley area, but the bucolic surroundings of the Catskill Mountains had not dulled his edge one bit. I found him in fine, bristling form!

JW: I'd first like to talk about your past, the beginnings of pub rock, and your seminal influence on the genre.

GP: You're a fat fuck, Weinerbaum.

JW: That's what my wife said this morning!

GP:—

JW: Can we talk about Brinsley Schwarz? I want to get that warm, oozy kind of roots rock, 1976 critics-only feeling you must have had when you first began playing with him. And the other Rumour guitarist, Martin Belmont (of the sadly departed Ducks Deluxe). What was it like working with him back in the Hope and Anchor days? Back in those great pub-rock days?

GP: I have a new record out. I've no interest in this bollocks.

JW: It's a very good record, Graham. But it must be very different for you without that beery, cozy, critics-friendly approach of the Rumour rhythm section, Andrew Bodnar and Stephen Goulding (of the sadly departed Bontemps Roulez). And what about all the problems you had with Mercury Records? My readers would love to know the ins and outs of that!

GP: Weinerbaum, do you have a file that says, Ask about pub rock, record-label problems, lack of commercial success, comparisons to other artists who came along "at around the same time" but were really a year after me, why did you split with the "sadly departed" Rumour, is "Can't Be Too Strong" really an anti-abortion song? Do you want me to go on with the fucking clichés, Weinerbaum?

JW: This is gold, Graham, gold!

GP: I know you, Weinerbaum. I've not forgotten that article you did in '77 when I stupidly allowed you to come on tour with us for four days of the most intense shit you ever saw on a stage and *still* (JW: GP's italics!) you kept calling us "pub rock," you fucking monkey!

(Parker refers to piece I wrote for the *Trouser Press* (now sadly departed) that ran in 1978.)

JW: Graham, I just wanted to capture that raw, rootsy, beery kind of home-spun London street cred—

GP: You fuck!

JW: I'm sorry if I didn't get it all right, but you and the boys drank an awful lot—

GP: Do think the Stones don't drink beer as well? Do you think *they* (Parker's italics!) didn't do their first gigs in London pubs? Do you think Bowie didn't do his share of pub gigs before moving on to theaters and all? Where am I playing these days, pubs?

JW: Well, the Chance is only a small step up—

GP: OK, OK, this is sort of a pub. They serve beer at any rate, but I played a college yesterday and...look, whatever, OK? The point I'm trying to make that you bifocaled fucking critics don't get is that I am a fucking rock 'n' roll star! I've been on "Top Of The Pops"! I've been on Letterman about seven times (JW: only four times at the time of this interview)! I am a fucking—a...a...

JW: (At this point there is some foam forming around the great pub rocker's lips. He does not look well, but I attribute this to the late evenings up drinking beer with the lads [unfortunately, not the sadly departed Rumour on this tour] and reminiscing about his glorious pub-rock past.)

GP: Weinerbaum, would you call the Sex Pistols a "pub rock" band?

JW: Well, no, they're a punk band, but—

GP: But they started in English pubs you asshole! That's where bands *have* (Parker's italics!) to start in England cuz it's the only place bands can get gigs until they've made it. Like I have, you twat! What rag are you writing this for anyway? *Trouser Press* is it? What's that tote bag you've got there? The one with what looks like a combine harvester on it.

(I turn the bag around and show GP the logo on the bag.)

JW: I'm writing this for *Camper's Monthly*, Graham.

GP: *Camper's* fucking *Monthly*?

JW: I had a minor breakdown just after I left the now sadly departed *Trouser Press*. It's common knowledge. I'm not proud of it, but it's no secret. *Camper's Monthly* are very interested in this piece. They're talking page four, where they usually put the very informative and well-loved compost-advice section!

GP: Weinerbaum? Weinerbaum? Is that really your name?

JW: Yes.

GP: I know my Yiddish. That means, like, "the sausage that grows on the tree," am I right?

JW: Well, almost. It actually means "the sausage that hangs from the bough."

GP: Look, you've ruined my career in this country with this pub-rock shit, do you realize that? You're an asshole that hangs from a fucking tree as far as I'm concerned.

JW: Gold, Graham! Gold!

GP: ?

JW: Now Graham, you've been described as an "angry young man," an "angry middle-aged man," and presumably you'll be described as an "angry old man" in the not too distant future. Would those descriptions be accurate? Are you angry?

GP: I'm certainly looking forward to being that old bastard on the bus who whacks people around the head with his cane for no apparent reason, yes.

JW: How many angry pub-rock singer/songwriters are there operating right now?

GP: Um, let me think. There are fifteen that I know of. There may be more, but there are a lot of guys who aren't really angry, they just wear loud shirts.

JW: I see. Interesting. Do you think Al Roker is just a fat clown?

GP: No, I think he's like a weather balloon or something. He's real accurate.

JW: (At this point in the interview Graham appeared to fall into a deep sleep, and then his road manager came in and rather roughly manhandled me out of the premises. But I'd got what I came for. A revealing talk with the pub rocker himself, and although his current band can't hold a candle to those [sadly departed] bristling pub-rock legends the Rumour, I couldn't stay in Poughkeepsie to see the show anyway. I had to get back to the city to meet the deadline for this piece. It was disappointing that back in '92, *Camper's Monthly* [now sadly departed] had more important issues to fill their pages with, but a great joy that now at last, Parker's [dwindling] fan base can get to read an interview with a great "press act" in full swing, no holds barred. This is Jay Weinerbaum signing out.)

MacTwiddle Thumb, Attorney

MacTwiddle's motto is "Judge Not". (Business is slow.)

Jillen Lowe

But the food won me over, as good food can do, and soon there were lots of things to love about being an upstate kid.

home-laid eggs

fresh peach pancakes

milk from a local farm

our neighbor's maple syrup

local bacon

The fall is my favorite time. Mom sold apples and rhubarb at the farmer's market, and I would start planning my Halloween costume.

For a kid, Rhinebeck Halloween requires planning and know-how.

HAPPY HALLOWEEN

An example of a good house.

RIP

When you're little, you have to be careful to avoid the bigger kids, who roam around with eggs and shaving cream.

And when you're older, you have to avoid the cops, who can catch you and take away your hard-purchased eggs and shaving cream!

Justice!

But it was always worth it.

pillowcase, to hold more candy

honey stick

Acknowledgments

Jack Kelly

WHERE TO START? Jimbo, my man, you were there at the beginning, when darkness was on the face of the deep. Remember that night, knocking 'em back, talking the talk, and you, out of the blue, go, "Why not write a book about it?" Who could have imagined where that one would lead, huh? This one's for you.

And to Derek T., who tends a mean bar at Zutty's Hideaway (2347 Highway 63 for those who want to quench a righteous thirst), if you hadn't poured us those Jägermeisters on the house, who knows? "Zounds good," you said. How many times did those two words ring in my ears as my finger joints, cramped with chalk, labored over the manuscript that quickly became a thing to love, a thing to fear.

To my editor, Olivia Gargantua, hand-holder, tamer of tempests, brow-stroker, oiler of troubled waters, ruthless cutter of my most black and blue prose, money-lender, discreet offerer of Kleenexes, who kept your head when all about you were losing theirs. Sorry about all the midnight calls, the three A.M. hysteria. Really sorry about the threats. Didn't mean them, even at the time—but of course you knew that. Olivia, morning star, fountain of wisdom, tower of strength, I couldn't have done it without you, comrade.

To Bill Faulkner and "Papa" Hemingway. On the shoulders of giants, right guys?

To my agent, Russ Rappaport, what can I say? Faith is a five-letter word, my friend. You were there for me when there was no there there, and don't think I don't appreciate. Your laughter when I first proposed the idea stung, I'll admit it. The times you refused to return my calls—the times you put me on hold after you called me—made me furious. But ultimately I found myself back at the keyboard banging out pages—I see what you were up to now, of course. Certainly I regret what I said when you told me about the advance. I now see that I'm not ready for the lifestyle changes that "big bucks" would have brought. I look forward with all my heart and soul to seeing this book, my book, our book, staring down at me the next time I cool my heels in your waiting room.

To the DeWitt and Lila Acheson Wallace Foundation, the National Endowment for the Arts, the MacDowell Colony, and the Writer's Guild Emergency Fund for the grants, residencies, loans, comfort, and support that you did not give me. What does not kill me makes me stronger.

Of course, to my parents. It all began in that creaking bed one night in 1974. Without your passing fancy, I never would have come into the world, never would have endured the toil of growing up, the ignominy of boyhood, all that. Without your backhanded encouragement, I never would have embraced the scrivener's trade. You who cut off of my allowance, who carped at me day and night, who piled my stuff on the front lawn—believe it or not, it was your stinginess that spurred me to take the "jobs" that provided so much material for this book. Thanks Mom. Thanks Dad.

I can't forget Mrs. Lewellyn, first grade, Walworth Elementary. Jump, Jip, Jump. See Jip jump. Remember, Mrs. L.? You opened the door and escorted me into the mansion of many rooms that is the good old English language. I can never thank you enough. I suggest you skip pages 1–12, 25, 86–92, and 215–307. In order to depict with fealty the world as it is, I had to use some language that you may find shocking, to say the least.

To Terry Gross, the greatest thing that ever happened to "National Public Radio," and to Oprah Winfrey, you are looking so good, girlfriend. Hope to be talking to both of you soon.

And then there's Lara, the late-morning barista at my local Starbucks. You'll never know how much those triple-shot skinny latte grandes contributed to what's written on these pages. And the similes I tendered about your eyes, your hair, the other parts of you—I don't think you ever appreciated them for what they were—messages from my heart. Your icy stare as you slid my java across the counter always said to me, "Get to work, pal, you've got deadlines to keep, and pages to write before you sleep." Yes, you too played a role in birthing this opus. And yes, it was I who slipped that fiver in the tip jar. You deserve it, Lara.

To Coach Van Spanker, who taught me that when the going gets tough, the tough really do get going! When you cut me from JV basketball, you could hardly have known that the NBA's loss would be literature's gain. I'm just sorry your dementia makes it impossible for you to know what I'm talking about, but from the bottom of my soul, I owed you big time, Coach.

And last but not least, to Beth. I guess you wish you'd stuck it out now, right, honey? No, don't go looking for yourself in these pages, you're not here. But, no hard feelings and I hope you're happy with your East Podunk McMansion, your Lexus, your liquid-crystal HD widescreen. Fact is, I really do hope life is treating you well, sweetheart. Sometimes, late at night, in spite of it all—in spite of your marriage, the two kids, the restraining order—I still think about what we had and how special it was. Call me. Please?

Suspicious Poem

Are you
really
reading
this
poem—
or
just
skimming it?

Sculptures

Sculptures are
growing larger.
Soon one will
fill Ireland.

Mississippi

Mississippi has
the softest
bowling balls.

Hot Dog

Farley Crawford

Suspicion Of Sanding

Denny Dillon

It was midnight. I stood on my porch in the moonlight next to a huge mint-green object: an antique dresser that I'd been sanding and painting since four. Looking up, I saw my neighbors peering out behind their curtains. *They think I'm nuts,* I thought, *a manic night owl working on furniture the color of a throat lozenge. A giant square pistachio. Why do they keep staring?! They better not call the police again! On what grounds?! Maybe I should quit for the night.*

It all started with Jeff, my handyman. I was struggling with an old farm table, trying to remove some paint with sandpaper.

"Try this," he said nonchalantly, handing me a tool I had never seen. It had a motorized, round sandpaper part that spun like a top.

"Take as much or little paint off as you want. Velcro the paper, turn it on, and you're in business."

"What's it called?" I asked innocently.

"RANDOM-ORBIT SANDER."

Those three words changed my life. I switched "on" and the paint flew off and my table transformed into Art. An instant antique. This tool was a miracle! It was easy, it was fun. I could not live another moment without one.

I drove to Home Depot, bought my orbit, sped home, and instantly started sanding.

First, my kitchen table, next a chair. Then bookcases, a bench, even my dog's water bowl. I felt giddy, riggish. I'd sand furniture, paint it "Society Hill Blue," splash on "Vreeland Green," and sand some more. Colors popped out of the wood like an antique puzzle.

My creativity soared. I didn't know I could sand. All I thought I could do was act!! This was better. NO MEMORIZING LINES. I DIDN'T NEED AN AGENT! Just different grits. High numbers made the furniture creamy. You could rub your face on it. I did.

People raved: "This chair feels like velvet!"

NO BAD REVIEWS! I smiled proudly, but remained modest.

One morning I sadly realized all the furniture in my house had been sanded. I had to look elsewhere. I flew to Texas and visited my friend's farm. Before unpacking, I found myself in the blistering sun, sweating like a crack addict, sanding three pieces of furniture. Finally I stopped; not because the humidity felt like a 500-pound woman was sitting on me; not even for the lemonade break she begged me to take; I stopped because I hated her sandpaper! It was primitive, the kind you clip on a wood block. I decided to treat her to a random-orbit sander. I hadn't thought to pack mine.

Despite her protests that we had a concert to attend, I convinced her to stop first at Home Depot. We were the only people in the chainsaw aisle wearing gowns.

Later at the concert I fantasized about sanding the violins.

Returning home, friends inquired, "How was your vacation?"

"Unbelievable! I sanded a pantry, footstool, and baseball bat."

I was met with looks of confusion and concern.

For awhile I stopped sanding. I put down my random orbit and went on auditions. But soon I started itching to check out used furniture stores for booty. I'd become anxious with palms sweaty and suddenly I was at Secondhand Stan's searching for wooden boxes. Maybe I'd find a credenza!

I bought elaborate sanders. Now I had three. Three sanders and no available furniture.

I feared I'd do something drastic. I started sneaking out at night peering into neighbors' houses to see if they had anything to sand. At parties, I'd make a mental note of objects in need of sanding at the home of the host. Should I advertise? Sander for hire? Steal furniture and return it after sanding? That's where the eyes behind the curtain come in.

It was a crisp summer night with sweetness in the air and I was empty. Three sanders on my workbench, stacks of sandpaper, and no wood in sight. I had to do it.

I crept over to their open garage and gingerly removed a stepladder . My plan was to "orbit," paint it "fancy chair yellow," re-sand, then return it. I wasn't stealing, I was *improving*. In my barn, I put blankets over me to muffle the noise. When I finished it looked 100% better.

"They could sell this," I thought, and snuck it back exactly where I found it. *They might suspect, but they could never <u>prove</u>.* I slept soundly that night.

The next day, just to be safe, I tossed my sanding clothes and paint, so I wasn't a bit nervous when a policeman knocked on my door.

"Have you noticed anything suspicious in the neighborhood?" he asked darting his eyes around the room.

"My neighbor has a pygmy goat. I find that suspicious."

He raised one eyebrow.

"May I look in your barn?"

I wasn't fazed in the least. My sanders were packed away, having their afternoon naps. He nosed around the ex-chicken coop shelves and noticed theatre paraphanalia.

"You look familiar.... Are you an actress?"

"Well, uh..."

Suddenly I noticed my white sanding mask in the corner. It had fresh yellow sawdust on the nose. I quickly changed the subject.

"You know this barn was built in 1840, they built carriages in it..."

"No kidding," he said instantly bored. "Well I should be on my way."

It worked. I played the historic card and he waved goodbye.

It was close. A brush with the Law. I needed to talk to someone. I drove to Ace Hardware in Rhinebeck because they wouldn't know me. I was a frequent sandpaper customer in Marbletown.

My heart pounded as I wandered through "tools." I noticed a young man gazing longingly at a random orbit.

"Do you sand?" I asked quietly.

"I used to. I gave it up. It took over my life."

I felt a kinship, a soulmate in sanding.

"I understand. I think I have a problem too. What do you do instead?"

His eyes met mine.

"I pray."

Driving back over the bridge his words echoed in my head.

"I pray."

"That's what I'll do," I thought. Peace came over me.

Seconds later I panicked as I pulled into my driveway and faced the trooper's car.

"Ma'am, we found a tiny boot print in your neighbor's garage and I remembered you had small feet. Do you swear you know nothing about this stepladder business?"

I blurted, "I'm sorry. I couldn't stop myself. I'm a sander!!"

All the way to the precinct I babbled in incomplete sentences about my "orbit fix" and "sanding blackouts."

They took my prints, but sawdust fell on the ink. They threatened me with trespassing until my acting skills awoke and I cried for forgiveness. I performed stand-up and promised an 8x10 if they would just release me. I was no threat to the community.

"You can go, but this serves as official warning against any suspicious sanding. Next time it's prison! You are allowed one phone call."

Thankful for privacy, I dialed ML. *She won't ask questions*, I thought, *and she owns a credenza.*

Joy Taylor

Forager

Peter Lewis

I T IS EARLY ON A CATSKILL SPRING MORNING. I'm in the woods, looking down, trying to decipher a brown mushroom from the brown tangle of the forest floor.

The man with me, my foraging mentor, my Virgil—call him Toad—has taken an intense dislike of me.

"Do you see it?" he wants to know.

"Not yet."

"There." He jabs at a spot about three feet away. "Right there."

I stare hard, offer up a little prayer. Still, nothing. Our quarry has eluded me yet again. No use fibbing a casual "Yes, yes, of course." Toad will make me show him.

There is an uncomfortable silence.

"Christ," mutters Toad. I figure he is going to take a swing at me.

I don't remember why I wanted to learn how to forage for the wild foods of spring. Fiddleheads are okay, but I like the idea more than the grassy reality. Ramps are great, but I know how to identify them. And though I dearly love the peppery assault of wild watercress, I am disturbed by the thought of it being bathed in giardia. It must have been the mushrooms.

I knew enough not to go lightly into the forage patch. There was no need to die at the altar of wild things so as to commune with them on a higher level. First I had to learn how to identify them. The false morel didn't get its name for nothing: "Scientists have found that the Conifer False Morel develops a compound similar to one used in the manufacture of rocket fuel," snickers the Audubon field guide.

A fellow in the Catskills was recommended. Foraging ran in his blood, I was told; he knew fiddleheads by species when they were only two inches tall, could distinguish between a ramp and a lily-of-the-valley at forty paces. The mushroom hadn't been invented that could elude his fungal radar. I gave him a call. As it had been a mild spring, we agreed to meet the last week of April on the upper Neversink River.

Toad bends over and slices off the morel at the stalk. I hardly need volunteer that the mushroom remained invisible to me until he had it in his hand. He holds it up for me to admire. I murmur something about the ribs and pits being Nature's gravy boat. Toad looks at me with a mixture of pity and contempt. He juts his chin at a neighboring valley, our next venue. He sheaths, I'm happy to note, his buck knife.

Morels can be hunted when the lilacs begin to open. They are one of those mushrooms taught to aspiring foragers, like hen of the woods and chicken of the woods and puffballs and the teeth, because they are identifiable, widespread, and choice. Jane Grigson recommends that you soak wild specimens in salted water to surprise any ants or other creatures lurking in the honeycomb. My cook wife, for no reason other than intuition, would rather give the mushrooms a good flick with the finger than immerse them.

The Catskill mushrooms being too furtive by half, my insecurities rise geometrically. I have a need to please Toad, to prove I'm no chump in the woods. Indeed, I like to think of myself a forest intimate, a latter-day waldgrave. I've had experiences—ecstasies—in the woods: I have spoken to trees, and they have answered; I have "run nood in the farst," though less said about that the better. Greek olive groves are my familiars, as are Connecticut old growths, relic stands in northern Scotland, the apple forests of Tian Shan, the maple-birch-oak community around my house. I say this not to establish bragging rights, though that's always important, but because I didn't say it to Toad. Which is probably my smartest act of the day, or my second luckiest. It wouldn't matter anyway. I am on his turf—here, now—and I look bad.

I turn my attention to more conspicuous quarry. The fiddleheads yodel. I whip out my Opinel—heavily burnished with use, a symbol of practical knowledge I flourish—and cut a few. I'm considering popping them directly into my mouth, for the brio and dash of it, when Toad comes up. "Bracken," he says, wearily. "Cancerous. You want to stick to the ostrich and wood ferns. Let's us stick to morels."

We silently top a rise and silently descend along a wooded ridge to what looks like an abandoned orchard, out in the middle of nowhere. Nowhere and somewhere change with avidity in the Catskills.

Toad stops. Glowers. "Do you see them now?" And an angel sings.

"Ah ha. There we are." A morel sits nestled among fallen leaves. Then another and another, every one of them transparent in their guilt, like crows sidling away from a shredded bag of trash: "Who, me?" My revenge is quick and simple and involves a knife.

Toad slaps me on the back, a gesture at once comradely and barely contained in its violence. Did I hear "pathetic" escape from under his breath? I let it pass, lost to the glory of the moment.

Kelcher On The Roof

Donald Rothschild

KELCHER WAS STUCK ON THE ROOF. Dressed in his brown coat and brown watch cap and with his round-shaped body, Kelcher looked like a bear. If a neighbor passing on Chestnut Street had looked up, he would've thought, "There's a bear up on Kelcher's roof."

The reason Kelcher was on the roof was the satellite dish. He had switched from cable to satellite in order to get a better deal on the flat-screen televison he had recently purchased. For six weeks everything had been super. Reception? Super. Number of channels? Super. Special features? Super. Now a day before the Super Bowl, without a cloud in the azure sky, the picture had gone out. Not so super. Kelcher had spent the better part of three hours on the phone yelling himself red in the face at various service technicians, but no matter how Kelcher cajoled, begged, or threatened, all the people he spoke with stuck to the same party line. Something must be interfering with the dish and the earliest a repairman could get out to Kelcher's house would be Thursday. Thursday? But the Super Bowl.... Didn't they understand the slow-cooked ribs Kelcher was marinating, the four cases of Blue Moon beer he was cooling, the family members who were descending on his house from points as far away as Buda, Texas? The satellite-dish people were all super sorry but there was nothing to be done unless...

"Yes," said Kelcher.

Unless, they said, Kelcher climbed up on the roof and took a look at the dish himself.

Twenty minutes later, Kelcher had jerry-rigged the kitchen ladder and hitched himself from the porch to the main part of the house. All he had to do was to climb up and over the top of the slate roof, and then slide down the other side to the south west corner where the dish stood aimed up towards the stars like a supplicant.

"This is the way," he thought. "Take matters into your own hands and solve them." He started whistling Springsteen's "Born in the USA." But as he climbed, Kelcher had the nagging feeling that he had forgotten something important. And when he peered over the side of the house to the steep drop down to the stone patio, he suddenly remembered. He was afraid of heights. Deathly afraid. Sweat instantly rose from every pore in his body and dripped down his sleeves and onto his hands. He started to slip backwards, picking up speed as he slid. He yelped out like a wounded coyote and dug his fingers into the slate to try and slow his fall, but there was nothing to grip. He was going over the side for sure. His life flashed before him like a cartoon and he thought, "I'm going to die." But just as his feet crested the gutter his coat caught on an old snow guard and held. For half an hour he yelled for help. Finally, he thought he saw his neighbor Nicolas Fleckston peering out from behind his curtains.

"Nicolas!" Kelcher cried. "Nicolas, please."

Kelcher and Fleckston hadn't spoken since the Ultimate Frisbee brouhaha two months before, when Fleckston and his brood had broken through Kelcher's fence chasing after their plastic sphere. Kelcher had built the fence between the properties last spring in protest against all the years of noise and squashed shrubbery; the hole in his fence was the last straw. He vowed never again to speak to Nicolas as long as either of them lived. He repeated this vow so often that his wife and two daughters stopped listening to him. Louisa, whom everyone called "Lou," was in the kitchen baking her award-winning pecan pie for Sally Fleckston, who was home recuperating from a strained buttocks she had incurred during morning yoga. Lou had continued to carry on normal relations with all of the Fleckstons much to her husband's chagrin. In fact, Kelcher was so angry with everything Fleckston that when he came upon one of their Frisbees in the street the night before while walking his mastiff "Poopsie," he gave it to the dog to chew to smithereens. Poopsie, apparently, was taking Lou's side in the feud and turned the other slob-wet cheek. So Kelcher was forced to chew on the Frisbee himself. But no matter how he gnarled at it, he couldn't tear through the plastic. In anger, he spun three times like an Olympic discus thrower and hurled the Frisbee into the heavens.

Now surely Nicolas had heard seen him hanging spread-eagled on the roof.

"Nicolas! Nicolas!"

But the curtains closed and no one had come.

Another half hour later Kelcher had gone hoarse from yelling when he heard Lou leaving the house carrying the pecan pie.

"Lou!" he cried. "Lou!" But his voice was no more than a whisper and Lou mistook his cries for the wind as she scurried across their lawn.

"That's it," he thought. Once they cut into the pie and started gabbing she would be there all night. He was doomed.

And then suddenly he heard a voice calling from below.

"Kelcher? Is that you up there?"

"Yes!" Kelcher croaked.

Now that they were back safe in the kitchen, Kelcher muttered the first words he had said to Nicolas Fleckston in two months.

"Thank you."

Fleckston smiled. Besides rescuing Kelcher, Nicholas had scaled over the roof like a Sherpa and in minutes had the satellite working like a charm. Kelcher knew he would owe his neighbor for the rest of his life and gratefully handed him a bottle of Blue Moon. Lou was finally making her way back through the hole in the fence.

"Please don't say anything," begged Kelcher.

Nicolas smiled and said, "You bet."

"By the way, what was the problem with the dish?" Kelcher whispered as Lou reached the porch.

"Oh, didn't I tell you?" Nicolas reached inside his coat and showed Kelcher the tooth-scarred Frisbee. Kelcher was still choking on his beer as Lou walked through the door.

Feng Shui for Complete Idiots

Cait Johnson

ENG SHUI IS AN ANCIENT CHINESE SYSTEM of interior placement and design that promises greater health, wealth, happiness, and pain-free joints, pronounced, not as any reasonable person would assume, but thusly: fung shoe-AY. Lately, many of us here in the Hudson Valley have been rushing about hiring feng shui consultants and paying perfectly good money for feng shui books because, after all, anything that offers such easy fixes for life's big problems sounds pretty attractive, right? I'm here to tell you: take it with a dash of soy sauce.

First of all, most of us are not Chinese (if you are Chinese, skip this bit). Imagery that may spell wealth to a Chinese person may not say much of anything to the rest of us. Take fish, for example. To the Chinese, fish are symbols of luck and prosperity, so if you put a goldfish in a bowl in your Prosperity area, it will attract wealth—or so the feng shui system would have us believe. Now I don't know about you, but I can't get a goldfish in a bowl to survive more than a couple of weeks in my house—maybe it's something in the Rhinebeck water—but I can tell you that there is nothing more depressing than coming downstairs in the morning and finding the latest in a series of goldfish floating belly-up in a bowl. It's enough to put you off your habitual means of making money for a month. And even if they somehow manage to stay alive and swimming, fish are kind of slimy. And, well, fishy. Sure, the gold color is pretty, but. It's all about intention, anyway, so rather than slavishly following Chinese precepts, and plastering your house with dragons and fish, you could strew dancing wombats or aardvarks around instead and get the same positive result.

Anything that focuses our intention (as self-help gurus have been telling us for years now) is a good thing.

Secondly, how many of us live in a square house? That's what you need for good feng shui. If your house is anything but a perfect square, your Love area may be sitting over your septic tank and doesn't that just say it all? Sure, there are "fixes" you can do to make everything dandy; but really, if your love life is in the toilet, plopping a wind chime or an eight-sided mirror with a little dangly tassel over the offending area just doesn't seem sufficient, somehow.

And, speaking of toilets, the ancient Chinese didn't have them, so there is simply no good place in the feng shui system to put your bathroom. Which means that all of us with indoor plumbing have our chi—or vital life-force—going merrily down the drain every time we flush or take a shower. So we're supposed to keep the bathroom door closed at all times (think of the mildew) or paint our bathrooms red, although somehow that never seemed like an optimal bathroom color to me and anyway, if the problem didn't exist for the people that invented the system, who's coming up with the fixes for it, I'd like to know? What guarantees do we have that they'll work? I refuse to go dig an outhouse just to be sure.

Now, I have nothing against applying basic feng shui principles to my home; I can feel the positive difference when I clear my clutter, and it feels proactive to light a candle in my Love area when the relationship chips are down. But I prefer to trust my own deep sense of what feels right, light, and good in my house, drawing on my own inner imagery-bank when setting an intention, and then stepping back and allowing the Mystery to do its thing, rather than relying on the lexicon of feng shui. But then, I'm a Western European mutt with a bathroom and an L-shaped house. If you're Chinese and you live in a square home (with an outhouse), go for it.

Country-Western Haiku
By Cora Sueleen Sprunt

Nina Shengold

GOOD EATS CAFÉ
Trucker sits. Orders
Adam & Eve on a raft
And cream, no sugar.

MISS CONGENIALITY BACKSTAGE
Miss Texas my foot.
She gave head to the judges
And can't twirl for beans.

DEATH OF A SALESGIRL
Everything Must Go
Read the sign in the window.
She read it and went.

HANK IS SO SENSITIVE
I know what you need,
Says Hank, taking his pants off.
You'll thank me for this.

DEATH ROW
Do Not Remove Tag
Under Penalty of Law.
We warned you, but no.

Business After Hours

"I'm weightless.
Oh, I'm under water.
Hey, I'm sinking pretty fast.
It's black...night.
Why can't I swim?
Thank God, the bottom.
Wing tips, jacket, vest.
Pants around my ankles.
Why am I holding this so tight?
Oh, shit, it's her bra.
Oh, shit, it's torn!
What's her name?"

THE LAST THING I WANTED TO DO was work that paddleboat around the lake in the middle of the night. Not only is a married man pressed for time, but feigning romance has its limits. Sticking to the formula, "you-sure-do-have-pretty-legs," and the never failing, "tell me more about yourself," usually does the trick. Clearly the voyage to consummation would be by paddleboat.

The paddleboat was an earlier refrain from Business After Hours in response to "tell me more about yourself." I feigned interest but my urges by this time in the evening went beyond listening to her résumé or learning about her hobbies. Like everyone else, I had a full day, buying and selling stocks and bonds, and had buttonholed nearly a hundred businesspeople at Business After Hours. Now that my marketing rituals at the earlier meetings were exercised and the hard core had adjourned to a "respectable" watering hole, it was time to cash in.

The cream had risen to the top. The setup was complete. We left.

Only two things bothered me. Neither was my conscience. No, one was her name. I didn't catch her name when it was first mentioned. When I said, I missed your name, she answered, "I like to be called 'Beaver.'" None of the implications from such a nickname contributed to my sense of well-being. In full rut, I decided to think about it after escaping at evening's end.

The other thing was her fixation with "paddleboat, moon, paddleboat, moon, paddleboat, moon."

There it was tied to a tiny dock ten paces from her condo door. I was going to have romance jammed down my throat whether I liked it or not. This was a bitter pill for a businessman simply trying to close a deal. Time was quickly slipping away, yet the last thing to do was let her know I was in a hurry and hope that somehow she wouldn't notice my keeping one foot on the floor. Better make the loop around the lake as quickly as possible.

Businessmen know when they are overdressed. Even in the dark I felt foolish floating in this child's toy in my school tie and dark three-piece suit. I loosened my tie. She wore a full-length dress, buttoned up, business attire.

We reached the middle. She stopped paddling and looked at me in the moonlight. I hadn't been listening. THIS was the setting that set her free. She unbuttoned her collar and I unbuttoned the rest.

I have to interrupt here to make a confession.

About twenty years earlier I had lured or was lured into a motel with what I considered a conquest. I was right in the movies, moving along toward the end of the beginning. "Take off your bra," I whispered.

"No, you take it off for me," she whispered back.

For some reason, reaching around her, I could not for the life of me get it unhooked. She at first whined, got impatient, then started complaining. The evening ended right there. After that incident, I tried to avoid the embarrassment of this incompetence with clasps.

Back at the boat, her clothes had flown off and there I was staring at the garment, causing over the decades so much low self-esteem.

Nothing, I decided would stand in my way. I gently grasped the garment's front in two hands and with a great burst of strength, tore it in two. Happily, the rending of the bra was seen as high passion. The paddleboat soon began to gently rock.

My focus narrowed at this point and I forgot some of the essential fruits of my high school physics. This well-known corollary of "natural frequency," I give to you right out of the book: "More important than the force with which you pump is the timing. Even small pumps or even small pushes from someone else, if delivered in rhythm with the natural frequency of the swinging motion, produce large amplitudes."

As you have guessed, a large amplitude was achieved and the boat went over.

It takes some time to regain composure after such intense focus. Options didn't occur until I hit bottom. The water was pleasantly warm and it was pretty hard to feel bad or look at the world pessimistically at that very moment.

A few seconds later, the view or lack of it at the lake's bottom was a different story.

Here, as I saw them, were the facts:

She is at the bottom of the lake.

Her clothes will be floating.

Her bra is torn.

We were seen leaving the bar.

I don't know her name.

I go directly to jail if I make it to the surface and she doesn't.

I learned nothing from Chappaquiddic.

But Beaver lived up to her name, surfacing with even more enhanced passion than that from the bra rending. We slogged to shore and her condo where I was able to keep one foot firmly on the floor.

Misfortune Cookies

Kent Babcock

So You Want to Live in the Country?

Jane Glucksman

DO NOT ARGUE WITH A MOVING MAN who is channeling Robert DeNiro in *Cape Fear*, especially as he is setting down your glass-topped coffee table. "Careful!" I wanted to shout as he nearly banged it against the door jam.

"You by any chance getting rid of that TV?" he wanted too know. His raspy smoker's voice and ripped prison physique complemented the assorted tattoos, which included the scary requisite teardrop under one eye. He stood outside puffing Camels during increasingly frequent breaks and stared at my house, nodding in some kind of vague approval. The guy getting his back was a tall black man, heavy and wide like a piano, whose stinky ten A.M. booze breath spoke volumes of the night before. He stood slumped in front of my brand-new side-by-side refrigerator, his giant right arm bracing against the top for support. This was not the opening-day, brand-new-life snapshot I had in mind.

"Would you like a glass of water?" I asked him gingerly. I actually thought he might pass out and watched in astonishment as he cupped his hands into the opening of the through-the-door ice maker and helped himself to as much ice as he could hold. He buried his face in his palms and sucked greedily for a few minutes, then unceremoniously dumped his leftovers into the kitchen sink. From that moment on, he disappeared in spirit from the moving job. Thirst quenched, he plopped his sweaty self down on my new leather sofa and soon thereafter asked for directions to the toilet.

Labor Day weekend came on the heels of moving in, and Sunday morning brought a surprise, a cold-call visit from a pest expert, a well-groomed man in a conservative, tidy beard dressed entirely in dark green permanent press. His crisp eccoutrement worked in his favor and served to evoke an authority of the natural world. I could picture him perfectly with a pet cheetah sidekick or a falcon perched on his fingertip. His company truck, parked in my driveway, featured giant insects with exaggerated menacing expressions, would-be perpetrators of a home invasion.

He asked my permission to come inside, and then he whipped out a clipboard with a thick wad of triplicate forms, which he began filing out, checking every single box. He was making excellent use of his hands; his right index finger slowly counted his left hand fingers, ticking off my potential enemies. I was spellbound.

"You have your termites, your roaches, your waterbugs, your wasps, your yellowjackets, your centipedes," describing for me in hairy detail the war against bugs, depicted as terrorists who could teach Saddam a thing or two about not getting caught. I wrote a check on the spot and made a standing monthly appointment, giving him a better time slot than my therapist.

During preparation for the inaugural dinner in my new home, the faucets went suddenly dry, and I grimly realized that there wasn't a drop of water except for a minute teaser of gravity trickle.

Oh plumber where art thou?

In our neck of the woods the week-long Dutchess County Fair is anticipated more than Christmas, and locals traditionally take time off to attend and then disappear fishing. Combing the yellow-page ads, I finally found a plumber who could swing by for a look-see.

"Yer well's run dry."

I was shocked.

"I suggest you use the bathrooms at the fair and let her build her reserves back up."

No washing, no peeing, no morning coffee.

"Potty!" my four year old wailed.

My resourceful mother, visiting from the city, took that as provocation to gather her wits and her purse and hightail it to the nearest Chinese restaurant to procure tonic for the Jewish soul: Moo Shu Pork (don't tell) and for good measure (or wishful thinking), Happy Family.

I prayed for rain.

Weeks later, Hurricane Floyd came barreling through.

Howling winds, sheets of rain. The lights were out, and I armed myself with flashlights and candles. I was hitting the wall while my kids bounced with excitement. The middle of the night drama was like a familiar situation they'd seen in some benign Disney movie where nothing ever ends too badly. Without power for heat, the house grew dramatically colder, and we huddled in a knot under the covers. In the morning I went downstairs to the basement to see if maybe there had been a miracle and I would find the boiler running. It was just a bad dream!

Instead, I stepped into a foot of cold rainwater. As my eyes adjusted to the windowless dark, my attention was drawn to a river of paper debris flowing, if not madly swirling, around me. Swimming in the soup were soaking-wet preschool art projects, the scratchy drawings of a toddler, a favorite Mother's Day painting with its primary colors now bleeding together, souvenirs of our family life I'd carefully saved for posterity. A birth announcement, my daughter's, sailed on by, its tiny pink satin bow limp and turning a bruised greenish color.

Who knew about sump pumps?

Enter my boiler man, punchier than usual in the wee hours before dawn. Moved by my unfortunate predicament, he waxed on about a happier subject: the good old days when he rocked out as the lead guitarist in a heavy-metal band. My imagination squinted to place him in schoolboy shorts a la Angus Young, but his habitual persona, underscored by the grease-stained jumpsuit, was pretty tough to shake. He fired up the furnace, testing its mettle, deliberately burning it to its threshold. It was like having a dragon in my basement spewing flames and bellowing a deafening roar: wild energy that caused my bed upstairs to vibrate. I pleaded my case: the noise was unbearable, the floors were shaking.

"Yeah," he said, "it's like being in a frickin' train station," his head bobbed up and down enthusiastically, in concert mode.

I concurred and shoved my bed across the room.

James Gurney

Memoir Mansion

Laura Shaine Cunningham

T HIS BROCHURE WAS RECENTLY FOUND, crumpled between business-class seats on the Amtrak "Highlander" train that runs along the Hudson River, transporting vacationers and "seekers" of solace to various retreats:

"Near Omega, and not far from Kripalu Yoga, is the discreet Memoir House, which caters to a specific clientele. A prerequisite for admittance is rejection by Yaddo and/or The MacDowell Colony.

"In Memoir House, there are many mansions. This discreet retreat for literary endeavor offers several unique accommodations. Located on a great estate in Edith Wharton country, Memoir House features distinctly varied chambers:

The Jean Rhys: Flowered wallpaper decorates this tiny parlor, which mimics a Paris bistro, offers a small table for one, and a limitless supply of Pernod. Not quite in period but within emotional context, Edith Piaf's recording of "Je Regrette Rien" is piped in continually. Tippling encouraged, and the occupant is expected to compose in longhand.

The Virginia Woolf: With a view of the Lighthouse, this octagonal turret room offers much to the sexually ambiguous and self-destructive. The vertiginous perspective is conducive to suicidal impulse, and a pre-stocked armoire offers a wardrobe of androgynous clothing.

The Marcel Proust: For those who enjoy the passive embrace of a male asexual literary presence, this brown, cork-lined study stocked with madeleines will take one easily back to "Temps Perdu." Check in is at 9:00 A.M. There is no check out time, but a minibar stocked with absinthe.

The Neurasthenic Lounge: No bed, only a chaise longue, for reclining with semipermanent undiagnosed nervous complaints. Equipped with side table for medicines and well stocked with such hard to acquire items as laudanum, smelling salts, and pure batiste linen handkerchiefs. Available for short or indeterminate long stays that may be extended into life expectancy. "Wasting" is encouraged, and all occupants report an average weight loss of twenty-two pounds, an unexpected benefit, somewhat offset by the advancing neuropathy of the feet. Limited use of "Vapors" spa.

The Jane Austen: For marriageable but still rebellious young women, who can chafe within its confines and spy, through a telescope provided, upon gentlemen who play croquet all day at the neighboring all-male Croquet Club. Tea is served constantly by slightly disgruntled serving women, and lump sugar is provided to sweeten the caustic dispositions within...

The Edith Wharton summer kitchen—otherwise known as "The House of Girth," the summer kitchen is stocked with "victuals" and farm-fresh produce, creamery butter, and Devonshire cream. Midnight snacking is de rigueur, and access to the kitchen garden invites midnight forays to munch directly from the growing fruits and vegetables. The summer kitchen is ideal for writers-to-be with hearty but discerning appetites, who wish to gorge selectively, expressing displaced sexual desires until the end of their stay, when a surprise awaits, in the form of a mysterious but well-muscled gardener. Late bloom is the name of the game here.

Check into Memoir Mansion, and check out with a book of one's own. The Enforced Solitude plan offers one meal a day and water in exchange for pages. Under Enforced Solitude, no one has failed to compose their memoir. Some have resorted to writing directly on their skin; occasionally in blood or other bodily effluents. If Enforced Solitude is too pressured, consider the more contemporary Late Harold Brodkey Plan—check in and out at will, with a pass to leave the grounds, readmittance acceptable for two decades, no need to complete anything. There is also the Lillian Hellman Plan—fabrication as an art form. High productivity is expected as one is not tethered to the truth.

At Memoir Mansion, one may encounter celebrities, in feeble disguises, perhaps with shaved heads; it is understood you will respect their privacy and not cry out their names as they strain to compose their own memoirs of abuse, addiction, and lives of entertaining degradation.

Danny Shanahan

REJECTION REDUX
(SEX, DEATH and KIDS)

"I thought maybe you could chew them off."

"I see a color and the color is red."

CAT 'O' LEMONS
$100.⁰⁰

Shanahan

Local Ills

David Smilow

"**O**H MAN."

"What's wrong?"

"I took a hike yesterday and I'm totally dead today. It's weird."

"Where'd you go?

"Up, uh...I can never remember the name of that trail. Devil's Pillow. Devil's Bolster. Something like that. It's an easy walk, though."

"You've probably got Lyme."

"What?"

"If you're so tired."

"Nah. I think I'm just getting old."

"You weren't getting old the last time you couldn't remember where you hiked."

"Plus I've been incredibly busy. The job. The other job. Carol. The kids. Trying to finish that stupid deck. I've been to Lowe's so many times they gave me my own red vest."

"Any joint pain?"

"Huh?"

"Like in the knuckles of your big toes. Do they hurt? Are your elbows sore? Your neck?"

"No."

"You're just getting old and tired. Aside from that, the body's perfect."

"Well, my knees are a little achy. But only a little. And okay, one shoulder's been kind of funky lately."

"Yup, Lyme."

"Would you stop? I don't have Lyme disease."

"Everybody's got it."

"You don't."

"Not anymore."

"You told me your test came back negative."

"That doesn't mean anything. My chimney guy—from Saugerties?—he told me this hotshot doctor he does work for over in Chatham told him there were more false negatives in the Hudson Valley than the rest of North America combined."

"What? That can't be true."

"So I guess you picked up a medical degree along with the pressure-treated while you were at Lowe's."

"I'm just saying—"

"You hear about the guy who went kayaking off Tivoli and fell asleep right in the middle of a stroke? True story. He just...drifted off. Literally. Came to at Mariner's Landing—you know, that seafood joint on the river just above the Mid-Hudson Bridge? The smell of fried clams woke him up. If not for that, he would've been out with the tide at the Verrazano Narrows. And guess what: His test had been negative too."

"Look, I realize there's a lot of Lyme out there..."

"A lot? There's no place it isn't anymore. Think about it: If you took all the tests that came back positive and added in the negative ones—which, like I say, are probably positive anyway—we're looking at close to a 100% infection rate, right? Mind you, that's just among the people who got tested. Imagine what's going on with the rest of the poor slobs who're walking around this valley clueless."

"So what did you do, take antibiotics?"

"Horse pills yea big, twice a day. In three weeks, all my Lyme symptoms were gone, including the most obvious one."

"Which was...?"

"Being absolutely convinced I had it."

"Well, I haven't reached that critical condition yet."

"Don't wait too long, pal. I'm serious. You don't take care of it, Lyme can screw up your joints permanently. Your heart. Your liver. Your brain. Your eyes."

"Your marriage. Your credit rating. The finish on your car."

"Go ahead. Joke. But personally, I think Lyme's behind a lot of the strangeness going on in our little corner of the world. It totally explains Spitzer."

"What? What are you talking about?"

"The guy gets elected by a landslide, he's all revved up, ready to clean house in Albany, only something's...off, you know? He's just not himself, after only a couple of months in office, and finally self-destructs. But why? It's crazy, makes no sense, any of it—until you picture that one tiny tick biting him. Yes sir. I say the spirochetes were running wild inside the man."

"You might want to consider another course of antibiotics. Your brain's definitely not what it should be."

"I'm telling you, this is nothing short of a plague! Cats have Lyme now. Dogs. Horses. Some high school kid's ferret came down with it. Lyme makes bird flu look like prickly heat. My firewood guy—from Mt. Tremper?—he told me about a baby that was born with Lyme. I swear. In Fishkill. There's even a name for it: Imils. I-M-I-L-S. Infantile Mother-Induced Lyme Syndrome. And by the way, you don't even need to be bitten by a tick anymore to get Lyme."

"Come on."

"I kid you not. A checkout lady at Adams told me some researcher at the NIH discovered pollen grains can actually carry the disease. Which means there's an 'allergen vector' to worry about now. So you can go for a hike—up the Devil's Duvet Cover, or whatever—and breathe in a friggin' case of the stuff."

"You aren't working for a drug company these days by any chance, are you?"

"They could use my help, believe me. Because I've got ideas."

"I've noticed."

"Top of the list? The State ought to provide free Doxycycline at all the rest stops on the Thruway. Have big bowls of it sitting right next to the bathroom doors. People could grab a handful of pills on their way out. Like mints."

"Just to be on the safe side."

"It's either that or wind up a bent-over, pain-wracked cripple with a bad heart and one eye gone."

"Only one eye?"

"I'm glad you think it's funny. Remind me to laugh when you can't zip up your own fly."

"All right. Maybe I will get tested."

"Don't even bother! Just get the drugs. Get the drugs."

"Hey."

"What's the matter?"

"The back of my arm. It's all red."

"Oh yeah. Wow."

"It's...it's a rash. I can't see all of it. Here. Look. Is it shaped like a bull's-eye?"

"Not really."

"What do you mean 'not really?' It either is or it isn't!"

"Well, it's got something of a roundish quality to it."

"Is it a goddamn bull's-eye or not?!"

"No! Relax, would you? It looks like a little poison ivy, that's all. Nothing to get all paranoid about. Jeez, get a grip. You'd think the world was coming to an end."

Opening Nights and Other Disasters

Lou Trapani

"H E'S NOT HERE!" our panicked stage manager shrieked at five minutes before curtain on the opening night of a major vaudeville piece I directed some years ago. She was referring to the "second banana" who figured prominently in the big number at the top of act 1. Thirty seconds of silence as all hearts in the dressing room ceased to beat, ended by the "top banana" turning to me and screaming, "You have to stall! Make something up!"

Easier said than done, Mister Top Chiquita Banana, I thought to myself and then began barking like a drill sergeant.

"Get me a pair of baggy pants," I ordered, "and an old derby, and a big bow tie, and some floppy shoes, and, oh yeah, let me have that eyebrow pencil so I can black out my front teeth."

All delivered in three minutes, I eased our stage manager in the direction of the tech booth and told her to shine the follow spot onto the center of the stage at precisely five minutes after eight and wait for me to come on. My plan was to grab a broom from the wings and treat the audience to the old Emmett Kelly routine. For those of you who don't remember, Emmett Kelly was the Ringling Brothers premiere sad-faced clown whose act consisted of trying to sweep a circle of light from the center ring. Every time Emmett swooped with his broom, the light would move away. A great and simple routine and I figured I could milk at least five minutes out of it and maybe even brazen it through to ten. I never got the chance to find out because at one minute to eight, banana number two arrived, apologizing for his late train, and scurried into costume. We only had to hold the curtain for three minutes, he scurried that fast.

Way back, my first professional opening night was of a very serious play, put on by some Cuban exiles, about a South American peasant who decides to carry a full-size cross on his back through 300 miles of steaming wilderness, into poor villages and town squares, in protest over...something. Actually, it wasn't a bad play and it had some pretty good speeches, but it was very poorly cast. I say this because I was to appear in act 2 as a burly(!), mustachioed, and very corrupt Latin sheriff who attempts to arrest our hero and prevent him from carrying his cross. I also say this because the kind and sympathetic village priest who befriends our hero in act 1 was being played by a very overweight and aging actor who had married a woman one-half his age but two weeks before (the woman was just a girl and not the kind of girl you take home to meet mother; rather, she was the kind of girl you take home to meet father). Apparently, the strain of this marriage, the strain of his too many pounds, and the heat of this particular opening night (it was mid-July, very steamy, and our poor theatre boasted not even a single fan) were too much for our village priest because he arrived at the theatre at half hour, young wife in tow, covered in a sheen of sweat and mumbling incomprehensibly. We were all more than just a little concerned but our priest waved our concern away with more mumbles and the kind of smile that makes one sensibly hide sharp objects and blunt instruments. But we needed to open this play (there was a critic among the two-score audience members) and there was no other priestly actor in site, so the show went on.

Well, things were fine for most of the act: Our hero hauled his cross dutifully, our priest said most of his lines (albeit shakily and with much outpouring of sweat), and the audience didn't boo or throw anything. As the act wound toward its conclusion, however, things got mean. Priest began saying things that simply were never intended to be part of the script and hero was taking this rather badly, particularly since the conclusion of the act was a very emotional (and actually well-written) scene between just the two of them all about life, death, the nature of the universe, and the crosses each of us must inevitably bear. Just before this scene was to begin, our priest turned away from our hero and stumbled to the edge of the stage. Pulling his many pounds as upright as he possibly could and sweating like Niagara Falls, he addressed the audience in an eerie voice.

"Ladies and gentlemen," he blathered like the madman he had become, "the basis of the theatre is improvisation. And tonight, I am going to improvise."

He didn't get very far because our hero (who just so happened to be the co-producer of this play and a bona fide revolutionary who had been smuggled out of Cuba after being wounded in some coup attempt against Castro) bellowed, "You son of a bitch!" as he hurled himself downstage and into our sweating, overweight, and over-married priest. Both priest and hero hit the floor, the curtain fell like night in the tropics, the twenty or so people in the audience (the lone critic among them) stumbled out of the theatre in shock, and we never did make it to act 2 or my burly, mustachioed entrance. This, by the way, is the only play I've heard of that closed before the first act even ended.

Renee Bailey & Sophia Tarassov

Multi-Cultural Greeting Cards

grassy-ass

mercy buckets

grât - z

tank - ewe

My Mistress' Ire

Laura Covello

"Art is a jealous mistress."
—Ralph Waldo Emerson, *Conduct of Life*

DEAR DIARY,
I blew it. Yesterday I was supposed to devote the entire day to my Art. (We were going to work on our screenplay.)

You know how she is about commitments. But Jack was feeling neglected, and I let him talk me into hanging out with him instead. "Tomorrow," I told my Art. "I promise." Big mistake!

I sat down at my computer this morning, bright and early, foolishly expecting the best. "I'm ready!" Silence. She wouldn't talk to me, not even to berate me for abandoning her. She completely froze me out.

I told her, look, he means nothing to me. He's just a guy. You're the one I care about.

But the screen's still blank. How can I get her to trust me again?

Dear Diary,
Thank God! I don't know how or why, but she's back. We spent the whole day writing the script. Bliss.

Dear Diary,
Can't she understand, I don't want to work in an office all day: Typing the boss's letters; answering the boss's phone; buying the boss's coffee and being

78

forced to call a small a tall—who would choose this? I would much rather be with her! I'm doing it for us!

I tell her this job pays for our studio—for the office nook we work in, for the bed niche we dream in. She scoffs.

She warns me that, one day, I'll come home to an empty screen and won't be able to fill it. She'll be gone for good.

I pacify her by promising we'll spend the whole weekend together. She's asleep now, but I can't get her threat out of my mind.

Dear Diary,

I screwed up, big time. It's the weekend, and I know I promised....But over breakfast, I found myself popping in a "Desperate Housewives" DVD—and then there I was, watching disc after disc, treating the whole third season like a bag of potato chips.

I tried to get her to watch with me: "Look at the brilliant plotting! The witty dialog! Remember how we were afraid it was ready to jump the shark? But it's better than ever!" Frosty silence. "These writers are masters," I told her. "I'm just watching for inspiration!" She didn't buy it. She left.

Dear Diary,

I didn't type a word—how could I, without her?—but I planted myself at the computer for the rest of the weekend, like Maggie Gyllenhaal in the wedding dress in *Secretary*. And, as with Maggie, it paid off! This morning, she relented. We wrote the big scene: The script got a climax, and so did we.

I'm off to work now, bleary-eyed. But happy.

Dear Diary,

She won't listen! She wanted to work on the screenplay, but I spent the day writing to agents. The business side has to be done—and, frankly, I don't see her doing it—so why the cold shoulder? Now I'm alone.

Jack called, but I ignored him. Anything to show her she comes first.

Dear Diary,

It was all my fault! We were doing so well—it was flowing like magic—when I...I....I can hardly bear to confess....I got hungry. I stopped—stupid!—just long enough to turn and open the fridge—it's right by my desk, like everything else—and grab the yogurt, which—I swear!—I ate right out of the container, in front of the computer. Working! Or trying to, because, in that one instant, she walked out.

Dear Diary,

Imbecile! After last week's yogurt fiasco, things were just getting back on track. But now...

I tried to ignore that "call of nature," but eventually I gave in. I mumbled a quick "excuse me," and was back from the bathroom in less than thirty seconds.

She was gone. Gone, gone, gone.

Dear Diary,

Wonderful, unpredictable....She's back!

Dear Diary,

I just looked at the clock. It's gotten dark. I spent the whole day at the computer—and, I just realized, I never got dressed. I'm still in my pajamas. And I'm so happy! Because she's happy. We're happy, happy, happy!

Dear Diary,

I thought it was such a brilliant solution. Jack was complaining he never sees me anymore. And you know how demanding my Art is. Since there's only one of me, and two of them, it finally hit me: "Let's all work on the screenplay together!"

Well. We tried. But it was so...stilted. Awkward. I know how to, you know, get him in the mood. And even her, sometimes. But both of them together? I was paralyzed.

Afterwards, we couldn't look at each other. And she's gone. Again.

Dear Diary,

Finally! I've won her, and I will be faithful. No more dating, no more temping; just the two of us—and our screenplay.

Dear Diary,

I did everything she wanted. How could she leave me?

Dear Diary,

You could say I'm screening calls, but that only applies if there's anyone you'd talk to. I can't get out of bed. Jack kept calling for awhile, but he stopped. Work keeps calling, but I can't even make up a lie and call in sick (again). I don't have the energy to turn on the TV, let alone the computer. I can only write this because I happened to leave the notebook within reach. All I can do is lie here, wishing she'd come back.

Dear Diary,

Jack dumped me via voicemail. I lost my job. The utilities were cut off, so the DVD player became a worthless relic. As did my computer. If an agent calls, and you no longer have phone service, does he make a sound? (No.) I'd still be in bed, but I got evicted. All I have left is this notebook.

Art now has my full and undivided attention. We're very happy, thank you. If you see us on the street corner, leave us alone. She wants me all to herself.

Economist's Sonnet

Mikhail Horowitz

SHALL I COMPARE THEE to a summer's capital accumulation?
Thou art more lovely and more fiscally considerable.
Rough deficits do shake the transition costs downplayed by
        privatization;
And summer's lease hath an all-too-short-term component of
        relative production to be profitable.
Sometime too hot the capital-wage ratio shines,
And often is the GDP deflator dimm'd;
And every deflationary tendency of the public sector over a
        procyclical period sometime declines,
By chance or the decoupling of relatively cheaper markets
        abroad untrimm'd;
But thy eternal liquidity shall not fade
Nor lose possession of that bubble mentality pertaining more
        to real estate than equities;
Nor shall Alan Greenspan brag thou depreciate in his shade,
When in eternal authorization by the Fed thou forecast a
        healthy, if not strong, rebound in overseas economies:
So long as men can breathe or eyes can see,
So long lives this, and this, according to Keynesian calculations,
        will initially have a negative impact on stock markets but
        will rebound in the third quarter and contribute a full
        percentage point to wage and salary income growth
        over the three-year period, leading to a consumer
        spending boom that should continue to rise and
        accelerate modestly.

Michael Maslin

SOME delights of The HUDSON VALLEY

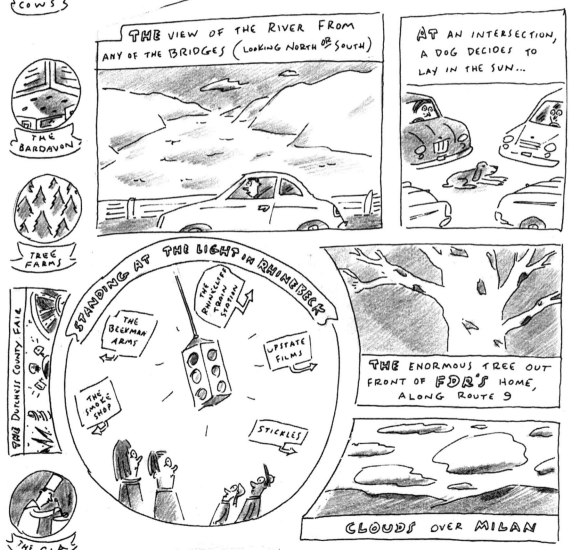

COWS

THE BARDAVON

TREE FARMS

THE DUTCHESS COUNTY FAIR

THE CIA

THE VIEW OF THE RIVER FROM ANY OF THE BRIDGES (LOOKING NORTH OR SOUTH)

AT AN INTERSECTION, A DOG DECIDES TO LAY IN THE SUN...

STANDING AT THE LIGHT IN RHINEBECK

THE RHINECLIFF TRAIN STATION

THE BEEKMAN ARMS

UPSTATE FILMS

THE SMOKE SHOP

STICKLES

THE ENORMOUS TREE OUT FRONT OF FDR'S HOME, ALONG ROUTE 9

CLOUDS OVER MILAN

Green Me

Ronnie Citron-Fink

ECO-TERRORISM IS A HARSH WORD. Maybe not eco-terrorism, maybe what I've staged is considered more like an eco-defense attack. I'll even entertain eco-crazed to describe what's happened. Either way, terrorism is more of an act against, and defense seems more appropriate since that's what moms do—defend. As a mom, the crazed part goes without saying. Anyway, I have to admit, I've dabbled in that underworld.

I became a card-carrying environmentalist by marriage. Believe me, I resisted for as long as I could. It's not that I would not have chosen this particular path or vocation; it's just that in the late 1970s and during the '80s when I was rooting around for a job, environmentalist wasn't on the list. Now it's cool and groovy to be labeled "green." Lucky for me, I can now pass for mainstream. It wasn't always that way.

The environmentalist label goes just so far. There is a line drawn between leaning towards being green and turning green. It's a spectrum of sorts. Let me explain how I leaned so far over that I toppled over the extreme green line, hence joining the ranks of the obsessed.

During my early adulthood, there were signs of what was coming down the pike. Maybe it was those people totting their doctrine, the *Whole Earth Almanac*. As scriptures go, this one was nothing to get all militant about. Plus, their footprints (and many of their heads) were in the sand. Except of course, when they wore the favored footwear—Earth Shoes. There were many fashionistas at the time that would have cited the wearers of these shoes as having a negative impact in those negative heels. They were some mighty footprints, but not of the carbon variety. The offense was purely a crime against the style-conscious. My compatriots and I from the Earth Shoe Free Zone of Long Island would never have been charged with that crime. Besides, I had just visited a college friend in New Jersey and Earth Shoes were all the rage there. No way, wouldn't be caught dead in them.

I can even remember when recycling was a choice. I used to go along my merry way picking and choosing what to recycle. I was convinced that the recycling, reducing, and reusing symbol meant a bicycle trip around the bike path to nowhere. At the time, I believe there was a map for that. I resisted the signs until I met my husband-to-be.

They don't call my husband, Ted, Mr. Green for nothing. Everything about his day job reeks of environmental garble. As an environmental planner, he is dedicated to "green" municipal planning. Actually, his Rhinebeck firm is called GREENPLAN. He has super powers and a super suit (under his bland khakis and blue oxford shirt). Really. Not only can he tell the future (acquiring his company name around 1990 and reaping the benefits for years to come) and track environmental trends, Ted approaches every aspect of his and our family life from a "green" perspective.

I should have suspected that he had a "green" agenda early on in our relationship. When I met Ted, he lived in a passive solar house equipped with a Clivis Multrum toilet. This was in the early '80s and one of the top songs of the year was a foretelling of the future. "Every Breath You Take" by the Police became the mantra in my new household for a cleaner environment. This is how it begins. First it's a benign "cleaner" environment. Before you know it, the whole family is reusing disposable plates until they biodegrade. Hugging trees with blind devotion became our religion.

Don't know what a Clivis Multrum toilet is? Well, let me just tell you it takes composting waste to a whole new level. Warming trends were felt first and foremost in that little solar house. The house was built entirely on bedrock on the edge of an idyllic stream. No septic. There was a huge tank for our upstairs toilet right behind a kitchen wall. I learned never to acknowledge that wall, and God knows what would have happened if you leaned against it. The most important rule regarding the Clivis was that the seat needed to be down when not in use for it to do its composting magic. I found out that a toilet seat left up on the Clivis could possibly lead to the demise of a beloved family pet. We almost learned that the hard way when our suicidal cat threatened to take the plunge after we exchanged his Cat Chow for Natural Planet Organic Cat Food.

Deep in the wonderland that is the Hudson Valley, Ted and I have raised our two kids. Their childhoods were seemingly uneventful to an untrained eye. On closer inspection, their environmental roots peeked out of their wings when they left the nest. Cloth diapers aside (such an environmentally charged issue anyway), they managed to fly off to their respective colleges unscathed by their parents' zeal about the environment. Once ensconced in their dorms, we knew they could easily change the light bulbs, lay down a bamboo mat, and take abbreviated showers. No one would be the worse for it. There was really nothing they could do about the formaldehyde-laden extra-long mattresses, except not sleep. I am sure college students don't sleep much anyway. I wasn't going to worry about it and compromised by buying them each a five-inch natural rubber (from a proprietary tree farm) mattress pads enclosed with hand–picked organic cotton covers. My daughter went to an art school. Eco-friendly furniture design was all the rage among the hip design students. Although I checked with the housing office once (maybe twice), the desks, couches, and chairs were made from nontoxic, sustainable, and they told me whenever possible, renewable materials. I was so proud of them when they weaned some of their friends away from those nasty plastic water bottles by converting them to using the stainless steel variety from the Klean Kanteen Company. For this reason, beer kegs are environmentally responsible. No problem there. Only once my daughter was asked if she descended from "hippies." She responded appropriately, by mentioning my aversion to Earth Shoes and leaving out her father's love of composting.

As Earth Day approached this year, and the fuel for my little diesel car (the biodeisel conversion kit is back-ordered) was getting astronomical, I knew Earth (and my pocketbook) needed more than a hug. I would have to leave my empty eco-nest and venture to the wilds of New Jersey to find cheaper diesel. At fifty-two miles to the gallon, it was worth the extra drive. As I veered onto the Thruway, I was escorted by truckers making their exodus to the border. My Jetta is like Mini Me to the truckers. They love me. We made it all the way over the line to my ex-nemesis, New Jersey. As I pumped that green gold into my car I couldn't help but wonder if the gas is always greener on the other side?

Deadlines

Delmar Hendricks

I AM IN THE NEWSPAPER BUSINESS—not a publisher nor a delivery boy. I write obituaries. Some of my subjects have been well known and some not known at all outside of limited precincts. Although it is a pretty interesting line of work. The outline of an obituary is fairly standard: age at death, occupation, surviving relatives, and outstanding achievements. But often there is a unique bit of information that can be worked into the article that makes it more interesting. For instance a left-handed violinist—now that's different. Or a man, who, in his boyhood, played jacks and marbles with his bare toes even though he was possessed of all his limbs and appendages. Or the lady author who did all of her writing in long-hand in green ink on pale yellow paper. Oddities can be fun.

At any rate, I do enjoy my work. Lately, though, I have been feeling signs of stress and my doctor says that I am reacting to the constant pressure of the job. Pressure is, of course, part of the newspaper necessity. If someone is caught stealing from his business, that information must be relayed to the reading public immediately; if someone plays a brilliant Hamlet, the word must be spread. Obituaries are no different—the only difference is that my field of writing gives a double entendre meaning to "deadline." So, my doctor advises that I find a pastime that I can enjoy and can relax with. I am pondering this when my wife, with whom I have been discussing the situation, says, "Marvin, think about gardening." I hate my first name and I hate the fact that my wife always can see solutions before I do and lets me know the fact. She went on, "Why not take a specific approach and create some breakthrough element of flowers or vegetables." A bit grudgingly, I reply that I will give this some serious thought.

I go to the library and check out some gardening books. Just reading them is pretty relaxing. But I need to concentrate on a particular area of horticulture for my restorative activity. I begin mentally sorting the various possibilities and come to "grafting." Now, that is something of interest. It's entirely new to me and appears to be something I might enjoy working at. The closest I've ever come to grafting was years ago when my dad was indicted for "graft" (no ing)—favors for favors kind of thing. However, he was able to "beat the rap."

Now, my kind of grafting will be strictly on the "up and up." I began going through possibilities. I first ruled out any kind of vegetable. I must work with woody plants and I further determine that shrubs or bushes are the more specific area of examination.

We're fortunate to have quite a bit of property around the house and lots of different plantings mostly provided by the previous owners. In my writing I usually emphasize the positive elements in my subject. So, that's my concentration on the established shrubs. There are bayberries—no, the thorns are too daunting. Rhododendrons: I have long taken a personal approach to them; I don't exactly have conversations with them, but I have given them non-botanical names that I use when pruning or fertilizing or just admiring. I can't see myself going to one and saying, "Now, Gretchen, I'm going to saw off this branch of yours and give you a new one." Deception would be involved since nothing is wrong with her branch and what if she wouldn't like the new one. No, definitely not the rhododendrons!

But I have quite a few viburnums. I think they may be just the thing. With the aid of one of my library books, I identify particular species and determine which ones should be compatible to proposed experimentation. None of them are in bloom right now. But my goal is to take a white blooming viburnum and a pink blooming one and create two shrubs with alternating branches of the two colors. The viburnum *carlesi* has pink blossoms and the viburnum *plicatum* has white ones. They branch out in the same manner and their branches have enough identical diameters to properly activate my ambitions.

Having chosen my subjects, I need grafting tools. They are closely akin to those used by surgeons. I purchase a finely honed cutting saw, a powder to be mixed with water that will speed up the healing joint where the old and new branches are joined, and "breathing" fabric to hold them together with a special botanical cord.

I bought a new journal to keep track of the progress made and also a new tape measure and a soft chalk for marking where the cuts will be made. Then special little tags for identifying and maintaining decisions made as to what goes where once the surgery begins.

It took me many hours to determine just which branches would match up with their new bodies by using the new chalk. The next day was Saturday. I did not plan to go into the office even if some spectacular death occurred.

The day dawned beautifully—a perfect day for concentrated (and relaxing) gardening. Out came the new elegant saw which positively gleamed in the morning sun. The first cut was precisely accomplished along the chalk line and that branch taken to its new home, which was identified on the tag. Then the cut on the receiving shrub, the joining of the branches, the application of the healing powders, and the binding with fabric and cord. I worked slowly and methodically and most happily.

To a passerby, the result of my labors must have presented a rather curious picture: two sizable bushes with a number of splints and bandages. Rather like an emergency operating area for the plant world.

I had followed directions and things seemed to be going well. Now began the waiting.

I was in constant attendance watching, admiring, expecting, making entries in my journal.

During these days, while not at work, I allowed myself to muse on bizarre obituary headlines. I liked to imagine titles to really grab the reader's attention. How about "Penelope Harvey, dead at 103 of over-age"? Or the victim of a hunting accident, "Edward Peters dies of faulty aiming." "Howard Evans, 88, seven times married, succumbs to overexposure." "Mary Andrews, 48, expires because of a faulty gas line."

Well, obviously I can't use those or anything like them, but it does amuse me.

Back to my viburnums. They continue to seem to be doing all right and I just keep checking and checking. This routine went on for a little over two weeks. Then one morning I arose and after a cup of coffee went out to check on my plants. I was horrified to see that an unpredicted freezing rain had fallen. All the trees and shrubs—including the viburnums—were completely coated with ice. I walked around my patients and, indeed, the covering was total. I couldn't shake them as the binding made them too vulnerable. I thought about applying hot cloths but I was afraid that might make matters worse. With a possible second shock—from cold to heat. No solution—even a remote one—occurred to me. I fretted about them for a good half hour and by then it was time to claim my desk at the newspaper. I spent a very anxious day there until I got home.

The day had brought warmer temperatures and the ice had melted some time before I stood before my plants again. They were a sorry sight. The splicing spots had all come undone and the graftings hung forlornly from the place of previous jointure. Furthermore, each of the host plants was damaged at the incised areas. It was a scene of death.

I won't enter into the dismal procedures of cleaning up the tragic remains. But there developed a bit of a silver lining. I wrote to the periodical *Horticulture Today* about my experiment. They are going to print my tale of woe, and knowing my daily occupation, for the first time ever, they are going to print double obituaries for my deceased viburnums.

Decoy

Jon Depreter

In Line

Molly O'Gorman

L IVING ON THE LOWER EAST SIDE in the eighties, I met with plenty of dog-eat-dog attitude. A typical creature of the suburbs, the only dog-like attitudes I knew were well-groomed and obedient. So what might happen when a creature from the burbs is removed from a sylvan setting and placed in a crowded chaotic city was revealed to me while waiting on line at the post office. It was a real life litmus test for behavioral science.

I had lived in other neighborhoods in Manhattan before moving to East Broadway, but nowhere was the absence of the venerable queue so painfully apparent as there. East Broadway is in the lowest part of Lower East Side, south of Canal Street. As you would find in most urban places, the simplest transactions there required waiting in line. In the mathematical theory of queuing, the First In First Out principle states that customers are served one at a time and that the customer who has been waiting the longest is served first. No problem. That's fair; you get your turn based on when you show up.

Well, on East Broadway you didn't simply wait your turn, you defended it. Lines there were hotly contentious turf battles where your survival instincts went into overdrive. There was no hanging, no zoning out, no messing around. You were one hundred percent alert at all times because if you didn't stay on the case some sneaky bastard would jump ahead.

Somehow I never adjusted to this quaint feature of the local culture and it never failed to drive me up a wall. Why did it have to be a competition? It's like haggling; I really don't get it. Don't give me all that back and forth routine.

It's not any fun for me, I don't enjoy it. Just tell me the damn price and take my money.

So one afternoon I went to the East Broadway post office; as usual there was a long, long dreary line. I took my place with casual resignation and waited as the line crept forward. About five minutes into the wait, a twenty-something Chinese fellow sailed in, daring a move so flat out obvious, so utterly indiscrete that no one seemed to notice. No one except me, of course. He stole directly to the head of the line with a seamlessly matter-of-fact air. A brilliant move.

I glared around at the other people on line searching their blank faces for signs of communal outrage. Surely someone caught this flagrant slap, surely someone would share my righteous indignation. Not this crowd, not one single person, not even one measly raised eyebrow. They all appeared to be completely and dumbly oblivious. But I just couldn't let him get away with it. I'd had it up to here with these local antics, this was the moment of truth.

Now in the '40s Hollywood version of this scene, I would have fixed him with a tart snap, "Why, the unmitigated gall!" Instead, in this scene my inner line monitor emerged out of nowhere. This newborn monitor hopped out of the line in high dudgeon and walked immediately up to Mr. Slick. An officious hand miraculously jutted up with palm wide open in classic halt position. Then in no uncertain terms, I fired at him in my best pidgin English, "STOP, NO GO." Keep in mind the visuals did not back me up at all. At five foot three and slight, I did not cut an imposing figure. Despite the lack of any serious physical threat, Mr. Slick heeded my pathetic command and fell into line with all the other drones waiting their turn.

Busted, Mr. Slick cleverly feigned an attitude of mild confusion, as though he simply did not understand English. Still I wasn't buying any of it. Where were the tokens of regret? No whisper of pardon me in any language passed his lips, nor was there even a shred of embarrassment. This was a polished act that had been performed numerous times before. But tell me, did he jump to the front of every line, or just some? And how often did he get away with it, I wondered? A hotter temper could really go off on a stuntman like that.

I was feeling pretty darn smug when I left the post office that day, like a bona fide upholder of justice. It was a coup of sorts, I suppose. It's been many years since Miss Monitor emerged and blurted, "Stop, No Go." And now that I live in the Hudson Valley there doesn't seem to be much demand for line monitors. Life is beautiful.

The Reading Channel

Sparrow

THE PROBLEM OF GROWING ILLITERACY in America is alarming. A 2004 study by the National Endowment for the Arts found the percentage of Americans reading literature has dropped dramatically in the past twenty years. A group called America Can Read! has a solution: the first Reading Channel on TV. Twenty-four hours a day, this channel will broadcast videos of people with books in their laps.

"Reading is reinforced behavior. One reason New Yorkers read so much is that they watch others reading, on buses and subways. In much of America, you never see anyone holding a book. On television, for example, reading is almost nonexistent. We want to return literacy to our national discourse," explains America Can Read! Chairman Pamela J. Semple.

Authur Plonge, Programming Director of the proposed channel, explains: "We'll present variations on a theme. Sometimes a young woman will be reading beside a glorious mountain vista. Sometimes you'll glimpse the title of a book—or even look over the shoulder of the reader and see the page! Or groups of people will read together, including families. 'The Family that Reads Together, Succeeds Together' is a title we're playing with.

"Or book races! Two readers begin the same book at the same moment. One is a Harvard professor, the other is a gang member from East L.A. Which one will finish first?"

Of course, the channel will be economical to run. "Also, there's a novelty factor," observes Plonge. "Viewers have seen every type of movie with special effects, every grotesque reality show—but they've never seen someone struggling to comprehend Bertrand Russell!"

For more information see americacanread!.com

Interview With A Name Artist

Sparrow

I SPOKE WITH LOCAL NAME ARTIST Ray Charlton.

Sparrow: I understand you're a name artist.

Charlton: Yes

Sparrow: How does that work, exactly?

Charlton: Call me a name.

Sparrow: Any name?

Charlton: Yes

Sparrow: Even a girl's name?

Charlton: Sure.

Sparrow: Okay. You're Amy Flanck.

Flanck: Great. Now I'm Amy Flanck.

Sparrow: That's remarkable.

Flanck: Now would you like to give me another name?

Sparrow: Sure. How about Edgar Widemann?

Widemann: Now I'm Edgar Widemann.

Sparrow: But you look the same.

Widemann: Yes. I'm a name artist, not a shape artist.

Sparrow: Can I give you another name?

Widemann: Of course.

Sparrow: Can it even be a non-word?

Widemann: Sure.

Sparrow: Even "&"?

Widemann: Yes.

Sparrow: Now be &.

&: I am &.

Sparrow: I think that's the last name I'll give you.

&: Fine.

Sparrow: So will your name remain "&"?

&: No. When you leave, I'll become Ray Charlton again.

Sparrow: I see.

&: But if you meet me at a party and call me "&," I will respond.

Sparrow: Thanks.

98

Three Degrees of Grief and Taste

Tom Davis

THE TOWN OF HUDSON HAS BECOME GENTRIFIED in the last thirteen years; Warren Street boasts several excellent restaurants, each with its own cuisine and ontology. The Red Dot may be the most colorful. The patrons are delightfully diverse and the discourse at the bar can be lively. I've made several good friends there.

The place is run by Alana Hauptman, an engaging woman with a wonderful laugh. She can be even more entertaining when she's not having a good day. She and Avis Davis have become close friends. He is an aging punk rocker who sold his loft in Soho ten years ago and gained a property overlooking the Hudson River and the Rip Van Winkle Bridge, a view that may have Frederic Church's Olana beat. Last Christmas Day, his beloved 115 pound black German Shepherd, Dark Prince, passed away at the age of sixteen.

Every person has his own way of grieving. After his old pal lay in state in a coffin on a bier on his deck, Avis spared no expense in having Dark Prince taxidermed (including the new dentistry) and had him preserved at attention in a lying position. The remaining remains were interred in front of the house, complete with an engraved headstone.

Frank Faulkner (a direct descendent of the author) is a regular of the Red Dot. He and his coterie can frequently be found at the end of the bar near the window looking out on the sidewalk. With his close-cropped hair and beard, and eyes that sparkle with intelligence and intensity, he is a successful real estate investor who meticulously restores old buildings and decorates them with museum-quality furniture and art.

Remember several years ago, Chicago had that lame-fuck idea to adorn their downtown with life-sized fiberglass cows, each painted by some worthy artist? Then, as if they couldn't come up with their own idea, New York City festooned the grassy medians of Park Avenue, and then several other cities followed suit. Last year, Catskill, Hudson's sister city across the bridge, put gaily decorated fiberglass cats up and down the main street. So this summer, Hudson decided fiberglass dogs would populate Warren Street and there would be a festival where dog owners and their pets could participate in a parade. The day came, and Avis was inspired to put Dark Prince on a platform on caster wheels. He and Alana pulled him along in the middle of the parade. When they got to The Dot, which wouldn't open until 5:00, they put Dark Prince in the window, and continued with the celebration. Frank was offended by this display, which he found tasteless, and after writing and signing a letter to that effect, he stuffed it under the door. At 5:00, Alana and Avis found Frank's missive, and they were offended, Avis being angered because Alana was upset.

The front of the house Frank is restoring had a couple of experimental patches of tasteful colors of paint so a proper decision could be carefully considered. That night, someone painted a swatch of hideous orange in this series on the front of his house, as if he were considering that hue. Frank did not think that was funny; however, a few days later, he and Alana made up.

Avis has specified in his will that when he de-animates, he will be taxidermed and set beside Dark Prince. Imagine that parade.

Dance

AbunDANCE

Dirk Zimmer

WHEN ASKED WHAT MADE ME STAY in the Hudson Valley, I usually answer the question in a very vague way or try to change the subject altogether. But since I have to answer with a written statement, let me be honest. Circa twenty-five years ago, when I was still a naïve and enthusiastic substance abuser, I witnessed the above scenery somewhere south of Olana and north of Germantown. It filled me with such awe and doubt in my mental ability to handle the situation that I turned away and decided to have a closer look at a later time. I tried many times afterwards to find the place again but it had vanished without a trace.

However, during my excursions I became quite intrigued—if not downright obsessed—with the sundry forms of local rituals and dances, which a patient explorer can still find in certain hidden corners of our wonderful valley.

Good RidDANCE

Confessions of a Deicide

Elizabeth Cunningham

I T ALL BEGAN IN MILLBROOK, NEW YORK, in 1956, then a sleepy Hudson Valley town with one traffic light, one cop, absolutely zero antique malls, and the usual three churches: Roman Catholic, generic Protestant, and Episcopal. In a small bedroom in the rectory of the Episcopal Church, the three-year-old, minister's daughter lay awake at night plotting the murder of God and Jesus.

That was me, and the murder plan is my first memory. I am able to date it, because I confessed to my eleven-year-old cousin who stayed with us for that summer. Her horror—"Say the Lord's Prayer! Quick!"–made the memory indelible.

How does a three year old go about killing Almighty God and his Only Begotten Son? My method was simple, really. I would go to the desert where they lived, the same desert where Wile E. Coyote was always trying to kill Road Runner. This desert, I knew from cartoons, had plenty of high pinnacles and sheer cliffs where huge boulders always seemed to perch precariously, just waiting to be tipped over the edge, to start an avalanche or to flatten whoever happened to be passing by below.

In this case: God and Jesus.

(Note: As for the Holy Ghost—yes, "Ghost" in those days; none of this New Age "Spirit" crap—I had the third member of the Trinity hopelessly confused with Casper the Friendly Ghost, so I wasn't so worried about him. But I do suggest someone conduct a serious study on the affect of cartoons on early childhood theological development.)

Back to the precipice where I waited poised behind the boulder watching God and Jesus floating over the desert below. God appeared to be an angry, black cloud. Jesus, inevitably, had long blonde hair and a long white robe, but no feet. He was God's son; he didn't have to walk. He and his father just drifted along, never suspecting that they were about to be flattened.

At just the right moment, I rolled the boulder over the cliff. A direct hit! God and Jesus went splat! But as anyone who has watched cartoons must know, the villain always springs back (with sound effects) from two to three dimensions. And so did God and Jesus (an early encounter with Resurrection), which was why I had to enact the murder scene over and over.

Until my cousin's reaction terrified me, and I went into mental hiding.

I soon discovered that any sort of concealment is difficult with a God who knows and sees everything—just like Santa Claus, and my two bald grandfathers in heaven. I was seriously outnumbered by omniscient males. (I remember my despair when it dawned on me I couldn't even have privacy in the bathroom.) If God and my grandfathers weren't bad enough, there was the further sinister fact that the one town cop (remember him?) was also named Mr. Cunningham, just like my father.

In some churches—maybe those other two—when people pray the Lord's Prayer, they say, "forgive us our sins" or "forgive us our debts" (a good prayer for everyone these days). But in the Episcopal Church, we say, "forgive us our trespasses," because we like words with lots of syllables—and maybe because Episcopalians believe in the sanctity of private property. I don't know if the Wings, who had owned the abandoned estate next door to the church, were Episcopalians. But there were No Trespassing signs all along the edge of Wings Wood.

How I found the nerve, as a fugitive deicide, I'll never know, but one day, I did it. I trespassed. I stepped over the wall into the wood with its huge trees arching over the crumbling carriage road. I even broke into the gatehouse—a tiny house with a turret and scalloped shingles that I had been sure were made of candy like the witch's house in *Hansel and Gretel*. The house was disappointingly empty, dusty, and void of magic. And that's when it hit me. I had trespassed. I had broken the law. God knew, and Mr. Cunningham the policeman was sure to find out. He would haul me off in handcuffs and throw me into jail forever.

I ran home where I had a sick migraine for days as I waited for Mr. Cunningham to come and arrest me. Though day after day he failed to arrive, I never confessed my trespasses to my parents.

And I never got over my terror of police.

It is more than fifty years since I plotted the murder of God and Jesus. I have moved halfway across the, uh, county. I have severed all ties to institutional religion. I have written heretical novels. I live in a wood where other people are the trespassers. (As long as they're not riding ATVs I don't mind.)

In the winter when it's hard to walk in the woods, I like to park my car and go for walks on one of the local back roads. One day I returned to find a message on my answering machine—from the State Police.

"This is Officer Allknowing calling about a 1997 Subaru Legacy found parked and abandoned on Pumpkin Lane. Please return this call immediately."

My hands are shaking and I break a sweat as I pick up the phone and identify myself to the officer.

"Is that your vehicle, Ma'am?"

(Why can't they just call it a car? Why do they have to call me ma'am?)

"I just parked it so I could take a walk," I somehow manage to speak, sure that I am about to be told I have committed a criminal offense.

"Oh, that's all right then," says the officer. "We just wanted to make sure the vehicle wasn't stolen or that you weren't in distress."

The policeman is your friend, I tell myself after I stop shaking. The principal is your pal. God loves you.

I think I will look around for a nice big boulder, just in case.

A Dog's Life

Nita Micossi

EVER SINCE THE GUINEA PIG DIED my husband has been leaning on me to get a dog. I knew I was in trouble when he insisted on selling the guinea pig's cage. "Won't need that old thing," he said. "It's time to move up!"

Then he brought home a half dozen library books about dogs including *We're Having A Puppy!*—a sensible and humorous introduction to the species; *Paws To Consider*—an honest appraisal of breeds that tells the truth about shedding and all-night howling; and *The Complete Dog Book*—a tome that extols the beauty and nobility of even the ugliest mutt.

My husband sat with our daughter, oohing and aahing over beagles, terriers, and bluetick coonhounds while I lost sleep replaying the comments of friends upon hearing the news of our impending blessed event.

"They bring in fleas, ticks, and dead rodents," warned Ada, a horse person, but emphatically not a dog person.

"They pee on your upholstery and spray the hardwood floors," said brother Jim, an unsentimental dog owner who knows my limitations.

"They eat feces," added his wife Betty. Gee, I'm glad you told me that.

Even the books—the honest ones—tell readers who want a dog to say good-bye to:

* Sleeping in on weekends
* Food without hair
* A dry toilet seat
* Spontaneous getaways

* White clothing
* Unbroken breakables
* Clean cars, and
* Walking barefoot

I don't even want to contemplate why I couldn't go barefoot in my own house anymore.

And what about the $2000 sleeper couch we wanted to buy so my sister-in-law won't have to camp out on the back lawn when she comes to visit? "How would you feel the first time the pooch pooped on your new $2000 sofa?" I taunted my husband.

"How will you feel about taking a puppy to your office everyday for six months until he's housebroken?" I threatened.

"What about my allergies to cats, dogs, and farm animals?" I wept.

But all he said was, "The kid needs a dog."

That's what my father said to my mother after my sister and I had left home and our younger brother was the lone child in the house. My brother frolicked with the mongrel he picked out at the pound. My father took pictures of my brother and the dog frolicking. My mother fed, bathed, and brushed the animal, brought him to the vet, and mopped up his hair balls and excrement.

This tale fell on deaf ears.

My husband continues to schedule appointments with breeders. My daughter is telling all her cousins that she is going to get a dog. Yet still I refuse to endorse this project.

Why? Why am I so adamant about living with a canine? Aren't dogs cute and lovable and loyal?

The truth is that I've always felt that whenever I've lived with a man it was already like living with a dog.

Think about it. A man sheds and expects you to pick up after him. A man must be fed and groomed and commanded to do something—or he will just hang out reading the newspaper and do nothing at all.

A man leaves the toilet seat wet. He chews with his mouth open and drips food on his coat. He growls whenever a stranger ogles his female. He needs to be petted daily and stroked behind the ears. And when a man likes you, he jumps up on your lap and drools all over your face.

Every man I have ever lived with had to be trained: when and where to eat, to not bark and disturb the neighbors, to heel when a girlfriend of mine he dislikes (or excessively likes) walks in the door. And I use essentially the same motivators as any good dog trainer: praise, food, and play.

Men are also prone to many of the same physical ailments as dogs. As one of the dog books points out, potential owners should beware of:
* Potbelly
* Bald patches
* Skin rashes
* Yellow teeth
* Snarling, and
* Discharge from the eyes, nose, or ears

That's pretty much the same list I gave to my cousin when she was out scouting for her third husband.

Not only do human males resemble canines in many ways, but human females often make the same mistakes with men as people in general make with dogs. For example, perusing *Paws To Consider*, I see the warning: "don't fall in love with a picture in a book." Alas, I'm sure I am not the only girl who has fallen for a scoundrel with a pretty face, to my everlasting regret.

And look at this: "You will know you are out of control when you leave messages on the answering machine for your dog and think the dog actually understands those messages." It took ten years of marriage before I abandoned all hope that my husband would read, let alone follow any messages I left on the refrigerator. And I know that the odds of a girlfriend getting a phone message from me are about the same whether I leave it with her husband or with her cocker spaniel.

Now I think dogs are okay. And I've had fond relations with two or three over the years. But do I really need to repeat a life experience I've already had more times than I care to recall? Besides, right now I already have a man in the house.

Do It
by Me

Nina Shengold

TO BE OR NO TO BE.

Ah! It is so... Ay me.

Si? No. Da? Uh uh.

Yo, do it, eh?

OK. K.O.

To do by ax.

Go up on el?

O.D.?

Et tu, Al, Ed, or Si?

(I'd be OK if he do me in,

Or do me. Ay yi yi, my id.)

No go. So nu?

Is it OK to be an un-me?

Hm.

Oh, ef it. I'm my ex.

Ta ta.

Restaurant Review

Tom Davis

La Petite Empriente de Pas Carbon *** [three stars]
Rhinebeck. French Asentient
$32.99 Prix Fixe

THE GREEN IDEOLOGY AND LIFESTYLE has increased the demand for vegetarian, vegan, and further dietary restrictions for those who will not eat anything with a face. Now Rhinebeck has a new restaurant to cater to these modern notions. La Petite Empriente de Pas Carbon is owned and operated by Chef Claude Lipowitz of Boston, and his wife, Cindy Alvarez, a native of Ancramdale. The two met as bioengineering majors at MIT who shared a passion for fine cuisine. They raise all the produce that makes up the menu, except for the organic grain, which is fed to the chickens, who are not eaten, but their manure is used to fertilize the heirloom tomatoes—recent blue ribbon winners at the State Fair. The tomatoes and arugula are raised year-round in Claude's closet using solar-powered grow lights and hydroponic irrigation using recycled paper hoses.

La Petite Empriente de Pas Carbon is the first restaurant outside of Berkeley, California, to raise faceless beef clones. These creatures have the normal bodies of cows, but their heads are about the size of a 4-wood, with single neck-holes through which feeding tubes from suspended bottles provide a constant source of pureed arugula and tomatoes. These asentient beings range freely, though blindly. When they are harvested, it is done as ecologically friendly as possible—with a blunt instrument. Nothing is wasted – the bones are baked and crushed to be used as fertilizer, and the hooves provide decorative finials for the restaurant's French Provincial ladder back chairs, and are available in the restaurant's gift shop. Even the methane is collected by balloons and tubes from the lower intestines, and used to fuel the restaurant's converted Viking stove.

Claude recalls, "I was raised as a reformed omnivore, but, in the summer of 2001, I was biking on a jogging trail when I was attacked by a bobcat. All my survival instincts came to the fore, and I killed the thing with my tire pump. I required 102 stitches to my arms and scalp, but I took the bobcat carcass home and ate it. The following morning I woke up a vegetarian." Cindy says, "I was raised as a vegetarian, but when Claude gave up eating anything with a face, he wanted me to give up something, too—so I converted to Judaism and now forgo oral sex." Cindy does indeed have a pretty face.

So, is La Petite Empriente de Pas Carbon kosher? Claude says, "Oh, my, yes—everything is blessed by Rabbi Hank Michaels of Temple Beth Shalom in Rhinecliff.

La Petite Empriente de Pas Carbon is located behind The Beekman Arms, in what was formerly the carriage house where George Washington convalesced from a bout of dysentery during the Battle of Saratoga.

La Petite Empriente de Pas Carbon is open for dinner Sunday through Friday from five until nine. Paper or plastic accepted.

Bushwhacking Buttermilk Falls

Elwood Smith

Dead Ringer

Jack Kelly

I NEVER THOUGHT THAT I LOOKED LIKE HIM, or like anybody else for that matter. Then I started to notice the way women were reacting to me. Strolling down Fifth, I would meet their eyes and they would switch on the 400-watt boogaloo. It gave me a bright, cosy feeling. A newfound Inner Magnetism, I thought.

Once a woman walked right up to me and said, "I love you!" I gave her my squinty appraising look. "Really," she went on, "I feel I know you. I'm sorry, everybody must be always—I'm so sorry." She blushed and hurried away.

Men reacted differently—a frown, a remark to a companion out the side of the mouth, a guffaw. I kept checking to see if I'd left my fly unzipped.

Finally I understood that I was the spitting image of one of the most accomplished actors of our time. I ordered all his movies from Netflix. I studied his mannerisms, his inflections, his squinty appraising look. I found myself acting like he acted in that one where he's falsely accused of murder and has to find the real killer, only he is not quite sure that he didn't do it himself in a trance or something. I felt persecuted. Edgy.

What's weird, big-time weird, is that before his career really took off he was in one of those straight-to-video low-budget jobs, where he played a pick-'n-twang mega-star named Hoot Farley. One day, behind a little too much Jack Daniels, Hoot hires an impersonator, who looks just like him and can sing just like him, to fill in at a gig. In the middle of the show, this stand-in Hoot has a large-sized coronary and dies. An outpouring of grief, a Nashville funeral, the works. Now what can the real Hoot do but pretend to be himself on the

Holiday Inn circuit? The high point is the National Hoot Farley Impersonators Contest. Who's going to win, the real Hoot, or a cocky kid who specializes in early, pre-beer-gut Hoot? I won't spoil it for you. All I can say is, I had me a few Jean-Paul-Sartre-at-three-in-the-morning shivers watching that one, pardner.

The more I became aware of the resemblance, the more I mimicked him. That little I-know-more-than-you-think-I-know smirk, that way he scratches his chin while bulging his cheek with his tongue. His persona began to impose itself on me. I don't normally say things like, "Cut off my legs and call me Shorty." He does. I started coming out with the stupid non sequiturs that are his trademark. "Hence the pyramids," things like that.

My girl took a long time to appreciate the resemblance, insisting that she just didn't "see it." I guess it grew on her, because she started to call me by his name. Only now and then, inadvertently, but it gave me a funny feeling. She got off on walking down the street and having people think she was dating him. I could feel her squeeze my arm possessively and knew she was hamming it up, winking at passersby. I began to wonder if what attracted her to me was my resemblance to him. Maybe she imagined it was him working the magic between the sheets. I grew jealous of him.

Cash in? Yeah, I admit I did film a couple of spots for a Dodge dealership on the Island, their end-of-season sellathon. They had me dress up like him in that famous role, the wild man who gets discovered in the New Guinea jungle and then turns out to be a mathematical genius. With the loin cloth and all. I felt silly.

More and more, the scene that keeps running through my head is where Hoot Farley's impersonating himself and crooning a my-baby-left-me song at the Elk's Club in Camden, New Jersey, and there's only about a dozen people watching, most of them soused. He's feeling kind of low, but then he spots this one woman, not glamorous or anything, and she's transfixed. She doesn't care that he isn't "real"—which he actually is, but she doesn't know it. It's just one soul touching another in the wee, wee hours.

So here you have me thinking about a celebrity for whom I'm a dead ringer, who's playing a celebrity who's pretending to be an imposter who's pretending to be himself, and who suddenly realizes that none of it means a damn thing because he's laying down some righteous tunes and helping a fellow human being make it through one more lonely night. Hence, as he would say, the pyramids.

James Gurney

Sandwich

Mary Gallagher

GOOD MORNING, ALL MY FRIENDS! I'm Rosario Rodriguez, you all know me, si? Ah, thank you, gracias—me, I'm delighted to see you too—all these smiling faces, eager to know and learn! So let's get started.—Jorge, are we set? Si? Okay, bueno, roll 'em!

Good morning, everyone! Good morning and welcome to our public access network program, "Sixty Seconds to Citizenship!" As you see, we're in the kitchen today, because today we're going to learn how to make the most central meal of the United States...a sandwich!

The sandwich can be eaten at any time of day or night. But its most frequent use is at the midday meal. This is because the midday meal is viewed in a completely different way here from in Latin cultures, where it is the most important meal of the day. "Almuerzo!" In Spanish, it's a word and a meal that you linger over...if you have anything to eat....

But in the United States, the midday meal is "lunch." You see? "Lunch!" You can tell just by the sound that you're supposed to get it over with. "Dinner," maybe you can take a little time. "Breakfast" even, maybe you can take a little time. But "lunch!" It's like "lunge," it's just one quick movement—like a dog snapping a fly—and then it's gone. And you keep working, working...and this is cultural. You see, in the United States, people believe that they should work very hard all day, on and on and on, and only think about their work.

And they're embarrassed to admit that they need to eat. So they hide their food between two pieces of square white bread—like this. Then it doesn't look like food. It doesn't even smell. It's just another envelope, it's anonymous. It could be a file folder. Or a pillowcase. You can hold it in one hand, casually, for hours if necessary, as if it doesn't matter anything to you. You might get around to it or you might not—it holds no interest for you, next to work. And with this type of bread, if you run into someone who will really disapprove of the fact that you need to eat, no problem—look closely here—you can squoosh it into pulp in one minute—gone!

Now you can fill your sandwich with anything at all. Watch now. Some meat or cheese...I'll put in both...some mustard and mayonnaise...or salsa or tahini...I'm putting on a nice layer of leftover frijoles, mmmm. You see? You can eat what you really want—anchovies, kim chi, manioc—if nobody can see it!

But! You see how these insides are now oozing and plopping out? No no no no no. Never overfill your sandwich. In the United States, food falling from a sandwich is one of the very few things that are seen as vulgar. Why? Because it shows greed—which by itself is not a problem—but along with greed, a lack of control. You took more than you needed, and YOU COULDN'T HANDLE IT!

That's our show today! This is Rosario Rodriguez saying, "Every minute counts!"

The Dutchess of Brassier

Phyllis Palmer

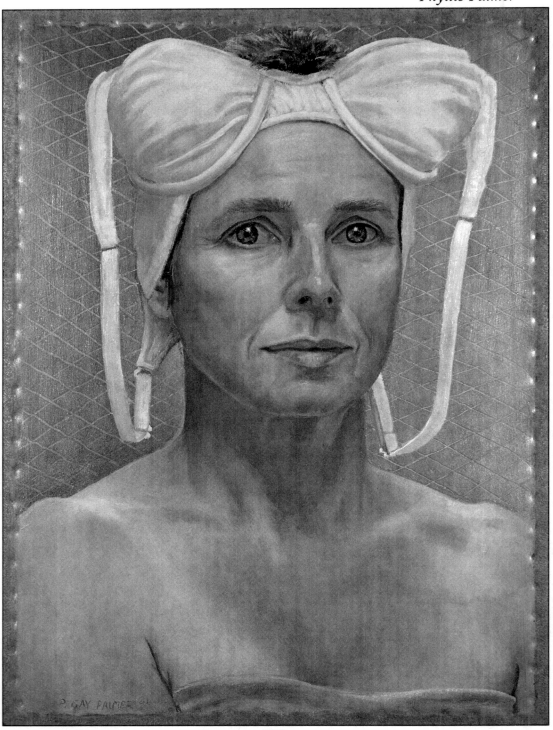

The Last Keggler

James P. Othmer

"On a level spot in the centre was a company of odd looking personages
playing at ninepins."
–Rip Van Winkle, by Washington Irving

"IS THAT THE GUY?"

"Do you see any other Keebler elves on my lanes?"

"I was just asking. And he's been what?"

"Using a little wooden ball."

"And?"

"Refusing to wear bowling shoes."

"Okay."

"And he's been taking away the freakin' headpin before he throws. Walking
down the aisle, which is totally against the rules if not the law, and carefully
removing the headpin, laying it in the gutter. Something very wrong, very de-
viant about that."

Wollman rolls his eyes. Troomp, the new owner of Kaaterskill Valley Lanes,
is a newbie. A city guy who came up here for the quality of life, then sets about
doing everything he can to change it. Ninety percent of Wollman's calls come
from newbies complaining about something that has always been, though he
has to admit, this is a little different. "Ninepins."

"Say what?" asks Troomp.

"He's playing ninepins. Old schoolin' it. Dutch game, I think, and no crime,
far as I can tell."

"Well he's freaking people out."

"There's no one else here."

"Maybe that's why. Look at his clothes. It took me fifteen minutes to get him to take the long knife out of the cloth thing on his waist and lose those shoes. High heels, with roses on 'em."

"Jerkin."

"I don't follow."

"On his waist. It's called a jerkin." Wollman stares at the little man as he saunters back up the lane after removing another headpin from the set. Straight down the center of the lane, like a ghost through the door of a dream. He reminds Wollman of something out of a Flemish painting, like the one behind the bar in the Keggler, the last building in town that hasn't been replaced by a nail salon or a video store. He's tiny. Maybe four feet tall. Long, red beard as thick as hemp. Large head. Small pig-like eyes with a huge nose. On his head is some kind of white hat from another era with a huge red feather stuck in the band. His pants are huge, covered with buttons down to the knees, probably woolen, which must not be very comfortable with today being July 3rd and all. Doublet, Wollman thinks, focusing on the man's snug-fitting, ornately buttoned jacket. How he knows this, Wollman has no idea but he's sure of it. The jacket is called a doublet. Just before the little man picks up his wooden ball he looks at Wollman and nods gravely. Not the happiest of elves, Wollman thinks, but he has to admire the way in which he goes about his business.

"So what are you gonna do about him? What are..."

Wollman holds up his hand, in effect shushing Troomp, as he watches the lone bowler in Kaaterskill Valley Lanes toe the line, cock back his right arm, and without so much as a step, release the ball. Not even the great Earl Anthony could have done any damage with a one-step, no-windup delivery, let alone a barefoot little person. But he does. The ball races down the center lane without spin or English and hits the ninepins with the force of lightning and the sound of thunder. Wollman looks at Troomp for some kind of validation of what he's just seen.

"Yeah," Troomp reluctantly says. "He's pretty good. But nobody wants to come bowl with a freak show like that here."

"How long has he been at it?"

"Since I opened. One strike after another. Whatever a 300 game is if you're using nine pins, he's done it more than once."

"Did he pay?"

Troomp digs into his pocket and holds out his hand. "May I?" Wollman reaches for the large gold coin in the palm of Troomp's hand. "He's paying you in gold and you're complaining? For three bucks a game he can bowl until next week and you'd still make out."

"I don't want his gold. I bet you he ain't even legal. And between you and me there ain't gonna be a bowling alley here next week. People can bowl in a video game. Why come here. I'm sellin'. Condos."

Wollman looks at Troomp. Wonderful. He decides that approaching the little man, no matter how strange the encounter might be, is preferable to spending another minute with Troomp. But first the cell phone in his trouser pocket rings. Or make that vibrates. It vibrates so powerfully it startles him. It is Becka, his wife. After a minute the buzzing stops but then it starts again.

"Yes, Becka....I understand Becka....As soon as I get home after this last call....It's the strangest thing....Okay....I respect that you don't care about my job, I guess....Do you remember when we had Jamie's birthday party at the bowling....Okay, I was just....No, no word on the promotion."

Click.

Wollman gingerly steps downstairs to the lane as if traversing a ravine. Another rumbling peal of thunder careens off the walls of Kaaterskill Valley Lanes, which are covered with faded murals of rugged, thickly wooded mountains, the hint of a fading river. When Wollman stands on equal footing with the last keggler the little man gestures for him to sit. In front of him, on the scorer's table next to an empty sheet covered with ads for places he wishes he'd never seen, is a flagon filled with a sharp-smelling liquor.

The little man has picked up his ball once again. Wollman turns and looks at Troomp, who is gesturing with both hands. C'mon! What are you doing?

Presently the phone in his pants begins to vibrate again but instead of reaching for it he reaches for the flagon.

As the liquid touches his lips all that Wollman can hear is the reprise of the little man's thunder.

Grandpa Woodstock

Jay Dorin

My Funniest Wildlife Stories

Annie B. Bond

M Y MOTHER WAS A STURDY PERSON, both emotionally and physically. She was no stranger to the natural world, in fact, she bravely welcomed the excitement that wildlife brought to our lives. She was entranced when we spotted a moose in New Brunswick, or when we saw an osprey at the ocean. So imagine our surprise when a mouse completely undid her composure.

Why my younger sister had a collection of white mice caged in her room I never asked, but one day when the cage was being cleaned, the mice escaped. Over the next few months our house held an expanding population of multiracial mice. We'd see them now and then, and worried about their ever-growing numbers. Well, everything came to head one evening when my mother was cooking dinner and a mouse ran up her pant leg! Once up the pant leg it began to race around on her leg itself, frantically trying to find an exit. My mother started shrieking and leapt onto a chair. It seemed that she had completely lost her mind, and we were relieved when she finally gained enough sense to stop the hopping and instead strip off her pants to release the mouse. At that point, seeing our mother on top of chair in her undies, my sisters and I were laughing so hard we were crying.

Then there was the time my husband Daniel exhibited temporary insanity when a bat flew into our big loft-like bedroom. It was a hot summer night when said bat entered through our imperfect screen in an open window. We both jumped out of bed. The frightful visions I had of my long hair becoming entangled with the bat were quickly put on the back burner when Daniel pulled our double bed mattress over his head—just his head, mind you, not mine—and ran yelling towards the door leaving me stranded in the middle of the room next to a box frame! A bit stunned, feeling like the plane took off without me, I finally adapted to the fact I had to take action alone, and ran to the door myself.

Flash forward about fifteen years. Our daughter Lily used to play the violin, and one night she was practicing in the living room when WHOMP, a flying squirrel landed on her shoulder. Everything became eerily silent as Lily stopped midnote and just stood there, stunned. I heard her father yell, "Oh, my God!" and then everything erupted into pandemonium as the squirrel leapt off of Lily. Lily started wailing, and the dogs went into an uproar chasing after the flying squirrel. I don't quite remember what happened next, but I think, after a bit more commotion, we took the dogs upstairs with us to bed and left the downstairs door open (a technique that had worked with an intruding skunk in my childhood). We never saw the squirrel again. Lily's violin teacher said that she had heard the whole gamut of excuses for not practicing, but Lily's won the prize.

As much as I love those memories, I think the wildlife story that still touches my heart the most, perhaps because we kept our composure, occurred during a family reunion in Maine. We were all sitting on a lovely cove beach—in fact, it was the beach filmed in the movie *The Cider House Rules.* My daughter Lily was about nine. There was a sign warning us to keep food covered and stored because of seagulls, which we obediently followed. The cove was beautiful and we spent the day playing Frisbee, braving the cold Maine waters, and lying in the sun. After a while we decided to have lunch, which we had made and packed in the morning.

Ocean air can make a person hungry, and it was a pleasure to settle down with our sandwiches. Suddenly, out of the blue, THWOMP, a seagull dive-bombed our group! Its beak was open and aimed at the sandwich Lily had in her hands, mid-lift to her mouth! The seemingly massive seagull snatched the sandwich out of Lily's hands and hurtled itself up and away into the air. Our jaws were hanging open, hardly grasping what had happened, when Lily's expression crumpled and tears started rolling down her face. She bemoaned the situation saying, "But I wanted that."

I've always thought of her decry to the seagull was as if she could reason with its unfairness, if somehow the lack of rightness could be fixed. No, it couldn't, but we of course all shared our lunches with her, albeit with a wary eye to the sky.

Laughing in the Valley

Robert Kelly

WELL, I DON'T HAVE ANYTHING FUNNY TO TELL YOU, but just look at me. A poet is always good for laughs. And I've been busy poeting in this valley longer than most. The angels talk to me, I talk to devils. People smile faintly and walk on by. People are, apart from American voters, inherently smart. Smart means: aware of self-interest and how to secure it. Don't listen to me.

The more serious he is (and poets take themselves very seriously indeed, since no one else does) the more ridiculous a poet is.

A poet, then, is always ridiculous.

A poet is an umbrella without a rainstorm,
a roadmap in the middle of the sea,
pork and beans without a plate,
a moon without a sky

an x without a y. You see what I mean, just fill in the rest.

But why aren't you laughing? A sobbing child is good for a laugh in this man's saloon. Little Nell croaking once again. Ronald Colman noble by the guillotine, it is to laugh. Everything is long ago.

Long ago is ridiculous. Time is a joke. On us. Or at least on me.

Long ago I stood one evening with Marlene Dietrich in the old Museum of Modern Art, when art still was modern. We were watching a retrospective of her movies in the theater downstairs. *Morocco*, was it? She played a spy, getting her comeuppance in front of the firing squad. On screen she was noble, cigarette-brave, a toss of the head, said her lines. The audience broke up with laughter, museums are so camp, kitsch looks exactly like kitsch, they all laughed. Marlene, standing at the back of the auditorium, burst into tears. They were laughing at her death scene. Why is this a funny story?

Are you laughing yet?

I think of Chanler Chapman, a distinguished eccentric, who published the *Barrytown Explorer* when I first moved into these enchanted woods. When I knew him, he was an old man, bent forward with age and eagerness, ever curious, upset, generous. His long patterned silk ties, fresh from the 1940s, hung to his knees as he scuttled forward. He cared about the woods, roads, toads, people even, and made quiet gifts to the poor. But what was ridiculous is that he ran a newspaper, a purely local paper, for and about the doings and doers of this corner of Northern Dutchess. It was as if the place meant something. As if people in a place were somehow, faintly, interestingly, different from people in some other place. As if place mattered. Isn't that ridiculous.

And it is still almost the most absurd thing about me: that I believe these noble hectares—say the terrain between the Roeliff Jansen Kill and Crum Elbow Creek, between the North River and the Taconic Revolution (those hills just this side of the Connecticut border)—to be radically and amazingly different from all other turf. Ley lines! Intersections! Whorls of selfic force! Dragon paths! Paucity of rattlesnakes, arrogant marmotry!
And if arrogant marmotry doesn't make you laugh, I wring my hands.

And does anyone actually know precisely how to go about wringing one's hands?

Biographies of Contributors

Kent Babcock's deep fascination and respect for the cartoon is one of his strongest early memories. "My first serious reading—all the works of Charles M. Schulz at age eight to ten—either turned me into, or revealed to me, myself as an existentialist, eventually a therapist, and perhaps, some day, just some kind of cartoonist after all."

Renée Bailey is a native of the Hudson Valley. She can be found in Ancram in her garden with a box of rain in one hand and clippers in the other.

Annie B. Bond (a.k.a. Berthold-Bond) is the executive editor of Care2.com's *Green Living* channels and authors *Care2 Ask Annie*, a tip-filled Q & A that offers practical advice on living green. She has written four books: *Home Enlightenment* (Rodale Press, 2005), *Better Basics for the Home* (Three Rivers Press, 1999), *Clean & Green* (Ceres Press, 1990), and *The Green Kitchen Handbook* (with Mothers & Others; foreword by Meryl Streep) (HarperCollins, 1997) and has been recognized as a leading authority, writer, and editor about the connections between the environment, personal health, and well-being.

Leon Botstein has been president of Bard College since 1975. He received his B.A. degree with special honors in history from the University of Chicago and M.A. and Ph.D. degrees in European history from Harvard. Dr. Botstein has been the music director of the American Symphony Orchestra since 1992 and was appointed the music director of the Jerusalem Symphony Orchestra, the orchestra of the Israel Broadcast Authority, in 2003. The author of *Jefferson's Children: Education and the Promise of American Culture*, he has been a pioneer in linking American higher education with public secondary schools. Dr. Botstein has received the Award for Distinguished Service to the Arts from the American Academy of Arts and Letters, Harvard University's Centennial Award, and the Cross of Honor from the Republic of Austria.

Mark R. Burns is a writer living in Rhinebeck, NY. He is currently putting the finishing touches on a theatrical play, two screenplays, three novels, and a salade niçoise. His most notable achievements include the screenplay for *Married to the Mob* (co-writer), eight years of teaching high school, and his three sons.

Laura Covello is an award-winning playwright who did *not* flee the city—but who found herself moving to the Hudson Valley anyway. Her work appears in the anthology *Women Forged in Fire* and has been read by Isaiah Sheffer on *Selected Shorts*.

Farley Crawford lives in a great lil 'hood in Kingston, New York where she oversees a small floral and vegetable jungle. She is an avid dog photographer and a traveler at heart. She tends a website of photographic and design work called www.stellaworks.com

Michael Crawford has been playing first base for the *New Yorker* softball team since Jackie left Dallas. In the off-season he lives, paints, and draws cartoons in the breakaway region just south of Rhinebeck. On the datatron he's at www.michaelcrawford.org and www.newyorker.com/online/blogs/cartoonists/michael_crawford

Biographies of Contributors

Elizabeth Cunningham is the author of The Maeve Chronicles, novels featuring the feisty, *funny* Celtic Mary Magdalen—who is no one's disciple. In spite of her early deicidal tendencies, Cunningham is an interfaith minister in private practice as a counselor. She has lived in the Hudson Valley most of her life. For more: www.passionofmarymagdalen.com

Laura Shaine Cunningham is the author of two memoirs, *Sleeping Arrangements* and *A Place in the Country*, both of which were published in the *New Yorker*.

Tom Davis is living in Livingston, NY. He huds in Hudson. He was half the comedy team of Franken and Davis for twenty years, and wrote at "Saturday Night Live" for twelve seasons, including the first five. He is proud not to have had a real job since 1970. A memoir, *39 Years of Short Term Memory Loss*, is to be released by GroveAtlantic in March 2009.

Jon DePreter's first memory was being bounced on a blanket by Native Americans at a fairgrounds outside of Fairbanks, Alaska, where his family was stationed with the US Air Force. He was two years old then. He now lives in Pine Plains with his wife Andrea, where he makes his wood sculptures and operates DePreter Designs, a sign studio. He has exhibited his artwork nationwide for over thirty years. His work can be seen at www.depreterdesigns.com or at www.elisatucciart.com

Denny Dillon is a Tony-nominated stage, television, and film actress. She won a CableACE Award for HBO's hit series "Dream On" and is an alumna of "Saturday Night Live." She made her film debut in *Saturday Night Fever* and was recently featured in the critically acclaimed *United 93*. A visual artist as well, Denny has an art gallery, THE DRAWING ROOM, in her 1840s farmhouse in Stone Ridge, where her whimsical pen & ink drawings and "art inside the box" are on display. Or visit her website: www.thedrawingroomonline.com

Liza Donnelly is a staff cartoonist for the *New Yorker*. Her cartoons have appeared regularly in the magazine since 1982, at which time she was the youngest and one of only three women cartoonists at the magazine. She has also written, edited & collaborated on numerous adult & children's humor books.

For **Jay Dorin,** being born in New York City was like being born in a living theater. He's lived in Clearwater, Florida, Miami Beach, Mill Valley, California, Ashland, Oregon, and then in a burst of sanity moved back to New York, finally settling in Rhinebeck with Lisa and their two-year-old son Max. It's now been fifteen years and all is well.

Ronnie Citron-Fink lives in Rhinebeck with her husband, two children (when they come home to the nest), her two dogs, and cat. She was a teacher and co-administrator at the Randolph School for many years. Ronnie was a contributing writer for *FamilyFun* magazine and her articles are included in three books, including *FamilyFun Home*. Currently, Ronnie works for Monkfish Publishing and writes a blog named *EcoNesting* for Care2's *Healthy and Green Living*.

Biographies of Contributors

Mary Gaitskill is the author of two collections of stories and two novels, the most recent being the novel *Veronica*. She lives in Red Hook with author Peter Trachtenberg. Gaitskill and Trachtenberg are at present working on a comic about the life of French mystic Simone Weil.

Mary Gallagher writes fiction, plays, and screenplays. Lots of her plays are published by Dramatists Play Service or anthologized. They're produced all over the US and in other countries. She's won a Guggenheim, a Blackburn Prize, and many grants and fellowships for playwriting, and the Writers Guild Award for screenwriting. She's working on a big, fat 19th-century novel and some short stuff in different forms.

Jane Glucksman lives part-time in the Hudson Valley. She is a writer, photographer, mother and real-estate agent. In her spare time she enjoys NASCAR and serves as chairman of the Brooklyn Heights Dachshund Social Club.

James Gurney is responsible for inflicting *Dinotopia: A Land Apart from Time* on unsuspecting readers in eighteen countries and thirty-two languages. He also practices the refined art of loitering known as plein air painting. He lives in the Hudson Valley with his two severest critics: his wife Jeanette and his parakeet, who claims dinosaurs in his family tree.

Jane Heidgerd received her B.A. from Bard College and her M.F.A. from the Milton Avery School of Fine Arts. In 2000, she received an award from the National Arts Club. Her chapbook, *Holy Cow*, was published by Deodora Books in 2007. Her work has also appeared in *Annandale, Riverdreams, Bullhead Books, Chronogram, First Intensity, Hudson Valley Magazine* and *South Mountain*. View her work at www.jheidgerd.blogspot.com

Delmar Hendricks began his professional life as a stage manager in the theater in stock, tours, off Broadway, and on Broadway. where his last show was the musical *Mame* with Angela Landsbury and Bea Arthurs. From there he went to Lincoln Center to perform a number of administrative jobs, but for most of that part of his career, chiefly as booking director of the two concert halls at the Center: Avery Fisher Hall and Alice Tully Hall. He also became interested in the visual arts while working with the permanent collection of sculpture and paintings at the Center and with a fine art poster and print program. He has made a happy transfer from New York City to the Hudson Valley and finds a great deal of his time involved with gardening activities.

One of the most vilified performers in the Hudson Valley, **Mikhail Horowitz** recycles literary classics, wedding them to blues, bop, hip hop, and other idioms, and also perpetrates his own stuff, namely New Age barroom ballads, recondite slide shows, and performance art pieces that begin and end in different geological epochs. He's the author of the collage opus *Big League Poets* (City Lights, 1978) and two volumes of poetry, and his performance work is collected on more than a dozen CDs.

Cait Johnson is a writer and counselor living and working in Rhinebeck, who, contrary to the views expressed in her piece, does keep a few dragons in her Prosperity area because you just never know, do you?

Biographies of Contributors

Jack Kelly has lived in the Hudson Valley for twenty years. He has written five novels, numerous nonfiction books, screenplays, and stories. His latest book is *Gunpowder: Alchemy, Bombards & Pyrotechnics*. He plans to try his hand soon at the most lucrative of all forms of writing, the ransom note.

Robert Kelly has taught at Bard College since 1961, and in recent years has been the co-director (with Mary Caponegro) of the Program in Written Arts. He lives in Annandale with his wife, Charlotte Mandell, translator of many French books, most recently Proust's *The Lemoine Affair* and Jonathan Littell's *Les Bienveillantes*. RK's recent books: a novel, *The Book from the Sky* out in October from North Atlantic, *Lapis* and *May Day* (collections of poems), *Threads* (long poem) and *Shame/Scham*, a bilingual prose text with Birgit Kempker.

Lucy Knisley, who has half-grown up in the Hudson Valley, is a graduate student at The Center for Cartoon Studies. Her first book, *French Milk* (Touchstone-Fireside) is out in October 2008. See her work at www.stoppayingattention.com

Peter Lewis works in the critically endangered trade known as geography. He is also a book reviewer, another species marked for extinction. Hence he lives with his family in the Hudson Highlands, way back in a hollow where bill collectors fear to tread.

Jillen Lowe was born in NYC. She raised two kids, worked as an advertising copywriter, was an owner/dealer of a Soho art gallery, and has been a journalist. She writes poetry, fiction, makes jewelry, draws cartoons, and lives in Rhinebeck.

Michael Maslin has been contributing to the *New Yorker* since 1977. A collection of his and Liza Donnelly's cartoons, *Cartoon Marriage*, will be published by Random House in 2009.

Peter McCarty is an author and illustrator of Caldecott Honor and Parent's Choice Award Winning book *Hondo and Fabian* He was living a happy life until he was forced to use a computer and color in his latest books. The agony of using computers and color can be heard in Clinton Corners, NY. Peter recently fixed the door to the garbage can without any help from his mom.

Me CV? Oy. I'm up in NY, OK? No ma or pa. If I'm on TV, so be it.

There are those who say that **Nita Micossi** has squandered her Ph.D. Her mother, for one. But Dr. M believes that thirty years of scribbling for all sorts of national and international rags—some sitting in your dentist's office, others known only to electrical engineers—has not only utilized her considerable skills, but entitled her to write anything she damn well pleases.

 Molly O'Gorman, a native New Yorker, currently lives in Rhinebeck, NY. She is the co-founder and co-owner of The July Group, an agency representing an international group of commercial artists and animators.

James P. Othmer is the author of the novel The *Futurist*, an excerpt of which was a finalist for the National Magazine Award in Fiction. His second novel, *Snipped*, and a memoir about searching for the meaning of life while writing dog food ads, will be published by Doubleday in 2009.

Phyllis Gay Palmer, being a painter and sculptor, especially of the figure, especially with her peculiar point of view, is not very practical. She doesn't seem to want to do anything else and after all these years she probably can't do anything else! She's lucky to live and have a studio in Tivoli.

Graham Parker, with his ace pub-rock band the (sadly departed) Rumour, broke into the British music scene with a vengeance in 1976, fueled on Parker's angry lyrics and the Rumour's good-timey R&B grooves. Since then, it's all been downhill. Having failed to capture a large audience, Parker and the Rumour parted company in 1980 and Parker has pursued a solo career ever since, playing to a shrinking audience of balding bespeckled gentlemen who constantly ask him if he will ever reform the (sadly) departed Rumour. Parker is now a bitter man, I know: I spent a weekend with him one night in San Jacinto where Parker, whilst eating dinner in a Mexican restaurant, grabbed a chimichunga and threw it against the wall after I asked him the dreaded "reform the Rumour" question. He is currently recovering in an upstate New York hospital after the biker at the next table, whose chimichunga Parker had thrown at the wall, gave him a comprehensive thrashing. —Jay Weinerbaum

Bill Richard is the youngest of nine children from Cream Street in Dutchess County. His career has been divided between teaching and financial services. After living in the Deep South for most of his adult life, he recently returned home where he says he sees it "for the first time." He now teaches at Marist College, provides financial services, and leads a Rhinebeck writers' group.

Playwright and screenwriter **Donald J. Rothschild** lives in Rhinebeck, NY with his wife Lottchen Shivers and his sons Sam and Gideon. Among his plays are *If Bet*, *A Duck in High Heels*, and *Shadow Bay* all performed at the West Bank Theatre in N.Y.C.

Wade Rubenstein is the author of the novel, *Gullboy* (2005, Counterpoint), which he wrote while living in the Town of Rhinebeck. If his characters sound familiar, be warned — seventy-eight percent of his life has been spent eavesdropping (the remainder on a bus, trying to get through Don Quixote). Originally from Wappingers Falls, via Brooklyn, he and his wife Mary are expecting their first child, a daughter.

Danny Shanahan has been drawing cartoons, covers, and illustrations for the *New Yorker* magazine since 1988. He is the author of four collections of cartoons, most recently *Bad Sex!*, published by Harry N. Abrams, Inc. He lives in Rhinebeck, NY.

Render Stetson-Shanahan is a 2008 graduate of Rhinebeck High School. He is currently a first-year student at Bard College.

David Smilow is a writer and actor and lives in Saugerties. He has written for—and performed in/on— movies, TV, and the stage. Locally, his...ahem...talents are most often on display with Actors & Writers, a reading-theatre company based in Olivebridge.

Biographies of Contributors

When **Elwood Smith** was born he was a baby. He had a large head and small, pudgy hands. He couldn't hold a pen. Now, he has a normal-sized head and he can hold a pen. He makes his living drawing funny pictures with his pen. He lives in the Hudson Valley with his wife, Maggie, and a deaf dog and three unruly cats.

Sparrow resides in a double-wide trailer in Phoenicia, New York (a hamlet of the Catskill Mountains), with his wife, Violet Snow, and daughter, Sylvia. He is reading the works of Freud—two pages a day. His latest book is called *America: A Prophecy* (Soft Skull Press).

Cora Sueleen Sprunt is the five-time runner-up in the Dallas/Fort Worth Cowboy Poetry and Twirling Contest. She was a finalist in the Sestina Special Olympics and the Flaming Pit Bar-B-Q Slam. Her poems have appeared in the *Perdenalles Review*, the *Waco Ghazal*, and the e-zine *Dismember the Alamo*. Ms. Sprunt (a.k.a. **Shengold**) is also the authorette of a chapbook entitled *Rode Hard and Put to Bed Wet: Erotic Tall Tales From the Land of Bush*. She is 1/17 Japanese, by way of her ancestor Hank-San, a Hairy Ainu from Lubbock. Read about her alias at www.ninashengold.com

Sophia Tarassov is a painter and designer transplanted to Millerton from New Jersey via San Francisco, where her creative energies are inspired by eggs, Spam, Black Sabbath, and iced coffee. A favorite fantasy is to run a pump trolley down the now rail trail. www.sophiatarassov.com

Joy Taylor exhibits regularly at BCB Art at 116 Warren Street in Hudson. She has a website—www.JoyTaylorArt.com—and she has lived in these parts since the days when all the restaurants were closed by nine on Saturday nights.

Lou Trapani has been the Artistic and Managing Director at The Center for the Performing Arts in Rhinebeck since 1999. He has been actively involved in the theater for over 40 years and regularly acts, directs, designs, produces, and stage manages. The CENTER for Performing Arts at Rhinebeck is a not-for-profit organization which is dedicated, through its arts and education programs, to providing arts experiences for people of all ages.

Mary Louise Wilson is an actress who won the 2008 Tony Award for *Grey Gardens*. She co-wrote the award winning play *Full Gallop*. Her articles have been published in *New York Times, American Theatre, The New Yorker*, and her plays in the one-act anthologies *Leading Women* and *Take Ten II*. She lives in Stone Ridge, NY where she acts, writes, and diddles around in her garden.

Dirk Zimmer grew up in Hamburg, West Germany, where he attended the Academy of Fine Arts during the 60s. In 1977 he came to New York City, started to work for newspapers and began writing and illustrating children's books. He lives in the Hudson Valley, sometimes on the west and sometimes on the east side of the river.

Jillen Lowe

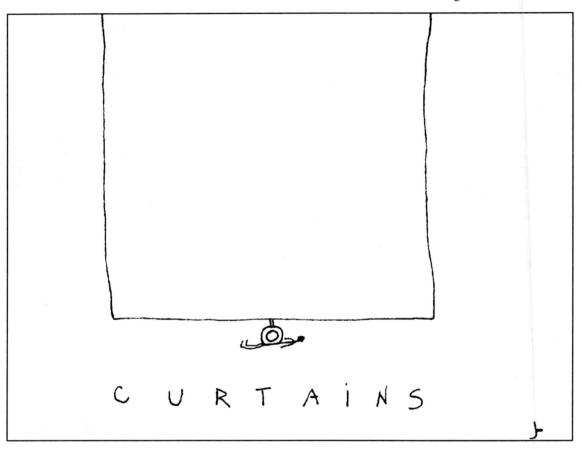

CURTAINS

Printed in the United States
205311BV00001B/203-524/P

9 780978 942748